Cataloging-in-publication data is on file at the Library of Congress.

ISBN-13 978-0-9830622-6-4

Photography: Edward D. Watkins
   as assisted by Carolyn Davis Pingree and Michael DeSanctis
Dave Cross Photography
Book design by Claire MacMaster, barefoot art graphic design
Cover illustration: ULC logo taken from a dinner program of the 30th Anniversary, 1893

Printed in United States of America

THE UNION LEAGUE CLUB

1863-2013

John Rousmaniere

THE UNION LEAGUE CLUB

Office of the
President

May 31, 2013

Fellow Members and Other Readers:

It is my great pleasure, in this 150th year of the Union League Club, to welcome you to this history of our Club. As you read these pages, I believe you will be inspired by the remarkable and lasting achievements of the Club and the members who have walked the halls of our Club-houses. That our first members would go to extraordinary lengths to help preserve the still young country is not surprising given that many of their grandparents had helped to lead the colonies and then the United States in its early days. Following the Civil War, this Club and the names of its members would continue to resonate through America's history as the country expanded its territories and influence westward and then globally.

I want to thank the author and especially the members of the 150th Anniversary Committee for their tireless efforts on behalf of the Club in connection with this book and all of the Club's memorable 150th anniversary events.

As a Club, we move forward with confidence in our third century knowing that the unique elements that have always distinguished our Club remain of great importance in today's world.

Sincerely,

David Mathus

David L. Mathus,

President

38 East 37th Street | New York, New York 10016 | 212 685-3800 | www.UnionLeagueClub.org

WASHINGTON, FEBRUARY 2013

Congressional Record

PROCEEDINGS AND DEBATES OF THE 113TH CONGRESS

IN RECOGNITION OF THE 150TH ANNIVERSARY OF THE UNION LEAGUE CLUB OF NEW YORK

HON. CAROLYN B. MALONEY
OF NEW YORK
IN THE HOUSE OF REPRESENTATIVES

Mr. Speaker, I rise to recognize the outstanding contributions of the Union League Club to New York City, the state and the nation on the occasion of its 150th Anniversary. At the height of the Civil War, the Union League Club formed with the mission of supporting the administration of President Abraham Lincoln to preserve the union. For 150 years, the group has been an example of the positive and enduring impact a group of concerned citizens can have on their community.

After the Civil War, the Union League Club amended its Articles of Association to say the Club would "resist and expose corruption and promote reform in our National, State and Municipal affairs, and to elevate the ideal of American citizenship." The members of this social club have played a role in the development of many historically significant institutions. Thomas Nast and other Club members were instrumental in bringing down Boss Tweed and eliminating the corruption of Tammany Hall. Union League Club members helped found the Metropolitan Museum of Art in 1870, one of today's premiere New York City treasures. Club members have also been involved in the development of other iconic institutions, including the American Museum of Natural History, the Frick Museum, the Julliard School of Music, the American Society for the Prevention of Cruelty to Animals (ASPCA), and the New York City Fire Department. Additionally, the Club's members have supported critical war efforts throughout history, and participated in fundraising for the base of the Statue of Liberty, the construction of Grant's Tomb and monuments to Abraham Lincoln and Admiral David Farragut, which stand in Madison Square Park in New York City. The Club supported the 369th Regiment of the U.S. Infantry during World War I.

Each year, the Union League Club honors two of its members with The Abraham Lincoln Literary Award and the Theodore Roosevelt American Experience Award. The namesakes for these awards reflect the Club's continued pride in its history, commemorating its original inspiration and one of its most illustrious members. Other Club traditions include sponsoring the annual

Thanksgiving dinner for the Soldiers', Sailors', Marines', Coast Guard and Airmen's Club in New York City and hosting wounded veterans and their families who come to the city to compete in the New York City Marathon and the Hope and Possibility Race in Central Park. The Club also provides educational scholarships for children of members through a charitable foundation.

Some of our nation's most famous figures have been members of the Union League Club. These have included 15 U.S. Presidents, seven Senators, many members of Congress, and other prominent officials in national and state government. The Union League Club has a distinguished list of past and current members, including: President Chester A. Arthur; Peter Cooper, philanthropist and founder of Cooper Union; Senator Chauncey M. Depew, U.S. Senator; William Evarts, U.S. Attorney General, Secretary of State, U.S. Senator and Chairman of the American Committee for the Statue of Liberty; Hamilton Fish, New York State Governor, U.S. Senator from New York and Secretary of State; Horace Greeley, newspaper editor and abolitionist; Charles Evans Hughes, Governor of New York State and U.S. Supreme Court Chief Justice; John Jay, U.S. Ambassador to Austria; Frederick Law Olmstead, designer of Central Park and Executive Secretary of the U.S. Sanitary Commission; George Opdyke, New York City Mayor and New York State Assemblyman; Nathan Miller, New York State Governor; Thomas Nast, political cartoonist and artist; Elihu Root, U.S. Senator from New York, Secretary of State and Nobel Peace Prize winner; and Charles Seymour Whitman, New York State Governor.

Mr. Speaker, I ask my colleagues to join me in recognizing the outstanding accomplishments of the members of the Union League Club. Throughout their 150-year history, they have made significant contributions that have shaped our nation's history and continue to benefit New Yorkers and Americans today.

Carolyn B. Maloney

CAROLYN B. MALONEY
Member of Congress

The Union League Club, 1863–2013

—

6

State of New York

Executive Chamber

Citation

Whereas, the Empire State is fortunate to be home to organizations founded in a spirit of communal and philanthropic service, and we join in recognizing The Union League Club on the occasion of its 150th anniversary; and

Whereas, The Union League Club was established in the midst of the Civil War by individuals concerned with preserving the Union, and committed to causes that would strengthen the framework of our society while improving peoples' quality of life; and

Whereas, over the past 150 years, The Union League Club's achievements have been significant and have had a profound impact on the United States and the social, educational, artistic, and scientific landscape of America; and

Whereas, thanks to the steadfast commitment and conscientious efforts of its members, The Union League Club has realized many accomplishments, including organization of the 20th, 26th, and 32nd regiments of the U.S. Army; organization of the New York City Fire Department; fundraising for the construction of the base of the Statue of Liberty; planning and organization of the Metropolitan Museum of Art; founding of the American Museum of Natural History and the Frick Museum; founding of the Julliard School of Music; founding of the American Society for the Prevention of Cruelty to Animals; founding of the United Sanitary Commission, which was forerunner to the American Red Cross; organization of the first Thanksgiving Day meal for members of the U.S Army in 1864, and the continuation of this tradition for all branches of service today; sponsorship of programs supporting Wounded Veterans, members of the U.S. military, and their families; and sponsorship of educational scholarship programs for Club family members; and

Whereas, today, members of The Union League Club continue to affirm their fraternal bonds and find fulfillment in working to improve our communities and make a meaningful difference in the world; and

Now, Therefore, I, Andrew M. Cuomo, Governor of the State of New York, do hereby confer this Citation upon

THE UNION LEAGUE CLUB

on the 150th Anniversary of its establishment, with congratulations to its members and best wishes for continued success.

Governor
February 21, 2013

The Union League Club, 1863–2013

The Assembly
State of New York

Proclamation

Honoring

The Union League Club

on its 150th Anniversary

Whereas, The Union League Club was established by a group of concerned citizens working to preserve the union and support the administration of Abraham Lincoln. The first of the club's original Articles of Association was to promote "unqualified loyalty to the Government of the United States, and unwavering support of its efforts for the suppression of the Rebellion;

Whereas, The Union League Club has devoted significant time and effort in helping establish and promote numerous civic, cultural, and military institutions at New York State levels;

Whereas, The club organized the 20th, 26th, and 31nd regiments of the United States Army during the civil war;

Whereas, Club president, John Jay, and other members recommended the formation of an art museum in New York City and were very involved in the formation of the metropolitan museum of Art;

Whereas, Club members helped found the American Society for the Prevention of Cruelty to Animals;

Whereas, Club members helped found both the American Museum of Natural History and the Frick museum;

Whereas, Club members helped to organize the New York City Fire Department;

Whereas, Club members drove the fundraising for the base of the Statue of Liberty;

Whereas, The club provides an annual Thanksgiving dinner for the Soldiers, Sailors, Marines, and Airmens Club in New York City;

Proclaimed, that this Legislative body pause in its deliberations to honor the Union League Club on its 150th Anniversary;

Proclaimed, that a copy of this Resolution, suitably engrossed, be transmitted to the Union League Club.

Dated: February 14, 2013
In witness whereof I have hereunto
set my hand and signature

Daniel Quart

Daniel Quart
New York State Assembly
73rd Assembly District

Foreword

I have enjoyed telling the fascinating story of the Union League Club's first 150 years and the people who played vital roles in it. I thank the Club for opening its comfortable Library to me and for the assistance of its members, especially Christine M. Rafalko, who represented the 150th Anniversary Committee and made me welcome. My thanks also go to the following for participating in interviews: John H. Farrington, James A. Jennings III, Sanwar Kashmeri, Allan M. Keene, Edwin F. LeGard, Jr., Walter H. Lion, Floyd W. McKinnon, James M. McKinnon, Marsha E. Malinowski, Jack A. Orben, Richard D. Phelan, Janet Ryder, Donald V. Smith, E. Nicholson Stewart, David Mathus, and Mary Beth Sullivan. I have benefited from attendance at meetings of Club committees and gatherings of old and young members, and from tours of the distinguished Clubhouse and its collections.

John Rousmaniere

December 13, 2012

READERS' NOTE:

Please note that we have strived for historical accuracy, so any direct quotes herein may contain misspellings or archaic terminology.

About the Author

John Rousmaniere's many books include histories of the Davis Polk & Wardwell law firm, the Equitable Life Assurance Society, the New York Yacht Club, the Evergreens Cemetery in Brooklyn, the Piping Rock Club, and other organizations, as well as histories and technical books on maritime subjects, including *After the Storm, Fastnet, Force 10, The Annapolis Book of Seamanship*, and *In a Class by Herself: The Yawl "Bolero" and the Passion for Craftsmanship*. He is a contributor to *The Encyclopedia of New York City* and *The Oxford Encyclopedia of Maritime History*. A graduate of Columbia University and Union Theological Seminary, he taught American history at West Point during his Army duty. He lives in Manhattan and is a member of the New York Yacht Club and the Century Association.

Acknowledgments

No project of the magnitude of a book, particularly one which seeks to recount 150 years of remarkable history and accomplishment could be achieved without the support and commitment of many people. The 150th Anniversary Book is the result of contributions by members and staff without which the book would not have been possible.

Work began in the fall of 2011 and continued under three successive Club Presidents, John R. Farrington, James A. Jennings, III and David Mathus. We appreciate their patience and support.

Throughout the process, members and staff offered strong support and greatly contributed with facts, pictures and other mementos, Edward and Austin Hayes, among them. To enrich and personalize the book as the Club's own, many members also agreed to be interviewed, including John R. Farrington, Richard Phelan, Floyd (Wink) W. McKinnon, Edwin F. LeGard, Jr., Jack R. Orben, James M. McKinnon, E. Nicholson Stewart, Allan Keene, Walter Lion, Mary Beth Sullivan, Marsha E. Malinowski, and James A. Jennings, III. Their time and generosity personalized the story as our own and for that we are all very grateful.

Many others contributed in many ways. We appreciate their support and the support of the Board of Governors. Several committees and other groups opened their meetings to the author, including the Rogues Lunch, and the Committees on Art, Library, History and Public Affairs, which provided the author insight into the activities of the Club.

The staff was superb and contributed in researching files and documents, opening the vault, and scheduling photography. Our thanks to the staff for their support throughout the process, especially General Manager Martin Hale, Sarah Simandl, Jessica Lyon, Kent Book, and Attila and his engineering team.

A group affectionately known as the Readers worked with the author and publishing team to develop the book. The Readers were David Ray, Franklin Ciaccio, Kimball Ann Lane, Marsha E. Malinowski and Christine M. Rafalko. Their unfailing dedication and commitment to the book as well as their love of history and of art resulted in what you hold in your hands today. Their meetings benefitted from the support of Ricardo Connell and Ricardo Bradshaw who made special efforts to ensure the Readers had what we needed.

To all of you mentioned here and to all the Club members who provided continued support and encouragement throughout the process, the Readers offer their most sincere thanks, for it is after all the members who make the Club and for that we are truly grateful.

Christine M. Rafalko
Chairman, 150th Anniversary Book Committee
July 20, 2013

Contents

The Founders

MEETING LINCOLN
"Every door has opened at our bidding from the President down," writes H. W. Bellows about the founders' close relationship with Abraham Lincoln.

1861

THE LOYALISTS' CLUB
The Club's founders step forward during the darkest days of the Civil War and commit themselves "to enforce a sense of the sacred obligation of citizenship."

1863

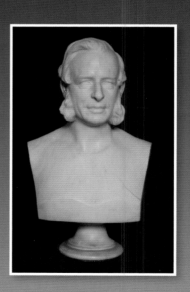

ROBERT MINTURN
This civic-minded "merchant prince" helps create Central Park and is elected the Club's first President.

1863

and Their Club

THE DRAFT RIOTS
The worst riots in New York history leave more than 1,000 dead. As the Clubhouse is attacked, members struggle to impose order.

1863

"OUR CLUB'S FIRST WORK"
"Colored" regiments sponsored by the club are presented their banners by wives of members and then march off to war in the South.

1863

REMEMBERING LINCOLN
Rumors and reports that the Confederacy was collapsing and in disarray reached New York in March 1865. Every night, the Union League Clubhouse, off Union Square, was packed with members reading telegraphed reports.

1864

HORACE GREELEY
The famous newspaper publisher and honored Club member triggers a national debate about Reconstruction when he bails Jefferson Davis out of prison.

1867

The Union League Club, 1863–2013

The Founders, Their Causes, and Abraham Lincoln

In order to understand the Union League Club of New York and its values, we should first know something about the founders and their world. The Club was conceived by a handful of vigorous, idealistic men who dedicated themselves to improving America in many ways, including the creation of two large, famous institutions: Central Park and the United States Sanitary Commission.

Today, three out of four New Yorkers live within ten minutes of one of the city's 1,700 parks, but before Central Park opened in 1859, the only land available for public recreation on Manhattan was Bowling Green and a few cemeteries. The movement to build a large public park was sparked by Robert Bowne Minturn, a ship owner who would be elected as the Union League Club's first President. After Central Park opened in 1859, its greensward landscape plan designed by Frederick Law Olmsted—another Club founder—set an international standard for parks that remains vital today.

Opposite: *Abraham Lincoln*
(Emanuel Leutze, 1865)

In May 1861, soon after the first guns of the Civil War were fired, the Rev. Henry W. Bellows, rector of Manhattan's All Souls Unitarian Church, co-founded a New York-based public health organization that rapidly evolved into the United States Sanitary Commission, the Union Army's and Navy's volunteer medical service. Called by one historian "the largest, most powerful, and most highly organized philanthropic activity that had ever been seen in America," this organization is described in detail in histories of the Civil War.[1]

Here our concern lies with its leaders, several of whom went on to found the Union League Club.

One was the Rev. Bellows, the Commission's charismatic leader. He once said that when he preached his sermons, it was with "earnestness and zeal which makes me feel as if I should fly out of my body, and they are listened to with an interest and silence which tells me they go to the right place."[2]

The treasurer of the Sanitary Commission was a highly regarded New York lawyer, George Templeton Strong, whose diary is one of the best sources on the early days of the Union League Club. A third Club founder deeply involved in the Sanitary Commission, in his case as a member of its medical advisory committee, was a well-known medical doctor and chemist, Oliver Wolcott Gibbs. It was Wolcott Gibbs who proposed the idea for the Club to the Commission's chief operating head, Frederick Law Olmsted—the man who had recently created Central Park with Robert Minturn, who was also an influential figure at the Commission.

When one of Gibbs' biographers mentioned his "strong, independent, and persistent character," he could have been referring to any of these men.[3] They believed that the United States needed moral reform, and they were not inclined to sit on the sidelines. After Bellows first met Olmsted during a tour of Central Park, he wrote an article for a national magazine praising the power of a well-planned institution to bring about widespread social betterment. The park was to Bellows a double sign of progress. The nation's business community can be a generous steward, and Americans will cooperate to benefit America by keeping "all that

has adorned and improved the past, while abandoning what had impaired and disgraced it."[4] Sharing these convictions, all these men took leading roles in organizing the Union League Club—Gibbs and Olmsted in proposing that it be formed, Strong and Bellows in establishing its aims, and Minturn in providing funds and structure.

Meeting President Lincoln

The Commission was formed, but it needed access to the Union troops, and that required a good word from Abraham Lincoln. Bellows drew on his son's friendship at Harvard with Lincoln's son Robert Todd Lincoln, and some contacts in New York, to arrange a meeting at the White House. The letter of introduction from a New York shipping magnate (and soon-to-be Union League Club member), Moses H. Grinnell, hinted at Bellows' entrepreneurial abilities: "The Doctor is alike eminent for eloquence, piety, and a large acquaintance with the progress of the age in development of humanity."[5] Bellows wrote home that he had enjoyed "an hour's very gracious and sympathetic intercourse with the President."[6] On June 13, 1861, Lincoln signed a bill creating the United States Sanitary Commission.

An unlikely but extremely effective relationship developed between the leaders of the Sanitary Commission and Lincoln. These were highly sophisticated, professional city men of Manhattan, and Lincoln was a country lawyer with a thick western accent and a style of rural informality. Early on in their relationship, Olmsted characterized Lincoln as "an amiable, honest, good fellow with no element of dignity, no tact, not a spark of genius." That initial patronizing judgment quickly gave way to respect and affection. Lincoln's "frankness & courageous directness overcame all critical disposition," Olmsted wrote a friend.[7]

George Templeton Strong was also won over. A trustee of Columbia College and an intimate of Episcopal bishops and men of wealth and power, Strong, like Olmsted, was initially taken aback by Lincoln's country ways. Presented with the proposal to approve the Commission, Lincoln complained it would be like

The Rev. Henry W. Bellows, a club founder, said of his forceful sermons,
"I preach them with earnestness and zeal."
(Daniel Huntington)

"the fifth wheel of the coach." When Bellows advised him to eat more carefully, the President replied, "Well, I cannot take my vittles regular, I kind o'just browse around." He explained his strategy of managing his quarrelsome Cabinet. When referring to his Secretary of War, he said, "Stanton's one of my team, and they must pull together. I can't any one on 'em a-kicking out."[8] Strong admitted in his diary that he and others initially underestimated Lincoln, believing him to be merely "a sensible, commonplace man, without special talent, except for story-telling," and even "a well-meaning, sagacious, kind-hearted, ignorant old codger." But he and the others quickly learned how wrong they were. "His weaknesses are on the surface," said Strong, "and his name will be of high account fifty years hence, and for many generations thereafter." Strong praised "our great and good President."[9]

Bellows triumphantly wrote his wife, "Every door has opened at our bidding from the President down all the way through the cabinet to the bureaus—and it would almost seem as if we had only to speak our will and have it done."[10] When the Army's Medical Department complained about the "strong-minded women" in the Commission's nursing division, Lincoln promised Bellows that he would identify "all the venerable do-nothings and senile obstructives that now vex the health and embarrass the safety of our troops." When elderly career medical officers protested that they were being shoved aside by the volunteer doctors, a bill

Abraham Lincoln and Jonathan Sturges (Club President 1864)
once worked side by side at this table, now in the collection of the Club. (Thomas Hicks)

In Lincoln's Handwriting

The Preliminary Emancipation Proclamation executed by Abraham Lincoln on September 22, 1862, is the only surviving known copy written in Lincoln's own hand. Lincoln later donated the original document to the Sanitary Commission, where it was raffled off to help raise funds for the war effort. Gerrit Smith, who won the raffle, then sold it to the New York State Legislature. It was later displayed in the New York State Library, where it remains today.

limiting the power of seniority was pushed through Congress and signed by the President. Lincoln instructed the generals, "The Sanitary Commission is doing a work of great humanity and of direct practical value to the nation, in this time of trial. . . . There is no agency through which voluntary offerings of patriotism can be more effectively made."[11]

In April 1864, the Union League Club elected President Lincoln as its first Honorary Member. A year later, Strong and many other Union League Club members were assigned prominent roles when the assassinated President's body was brought to New York on the great funeral train.

Lincoln at the Union League Club

Abraham Lincoln is handsomely represented at the Union League Club in many works of art—portraits, other paintings, drawings, studies, and busts. In the lobby is a bust of Lincoln presented by Leo Cherne (miniatures of this bust are awarded to speakers at the Club). Another Lincoln bust, in the Library, is by Max Bachmann, a German-born artist also noted for his noble busts

of American Indians. Around the time the Bachmann bust was acquired in 1955, the Club's Great Hall, where meetings are held, was renamed Lincoln Hall. Another of the Club's treasures is a table at which Lincoln and the Club's second President, Jonathan Sturges, had worked together when Lincoln represented a railroad of which Sturges was an officer.

Lincoln is the subject of one of the most imposing paintings in the Clubhouse, the nearly full-length portrait, titled *Lincoln Taking the Oath of Office on the Steps of the United States Capital*, displayed in Lincoln Hall. The artist is Emanuel Leutze, the German-American painter famous for *Washington Crossing the Delaware*. Based on a photograph by Matthew Brady, the painting was completed in 1865 and acquired by the Club for $500 in 1886.

President Sturges was a founder of the Club's art collection and father-in-law of longtime member J. Pierpont Morgan. (Daniel Huntington)

A Copperhead City

In the history he wrote of the Club in 1879, Henry W. Bellows sketched out how the men of the Sanitary Commission helped create a second institution in the midst of the Civil War: "These men were compelled during the war to pass some part of each day or night in conference with each other upon the urgent and anxious business that engaged them."[12] The tight bonds formed by these energetic idealists of diverse backgrounds inevitably led in a new direction. The initiative to form a permanent institution was taken by the chemist in the group, Wolcott Gibbs. In October 1862, he wrote to Frederick Law Olmsted proposing that they and their colleagues and friends found a national organization called "The Loyalist's Club."[13]

"Loyalty" was the highest ideal for Republicans and other Unionists who supported the war and Lincoln. His promulgation of the Emancipation Proclamation had triggered cries of "Washington despotism" from the many opponents of the War in New York. While Mayor Fernando Wood proposed that New York become an international "open city," Horatio Seymour successfully ran for governor on a platform that included a demand that New York secede from the Union. Gibbs and Olmsted met to identify the men they wanted to see as members. After many more meetings by an expanding circle, the Club came into existence in February 1863 under a different name and with such a burst of hope and promise that the founding agreement was sometimes referred to as "The Union League Covenant."

Opposite: *The Wounded Drummer Boy*
(Eastman Johnson, 1891)

"The founders felt that this was not to be a mere social organization," remembered founding member Harry Crews. "There were vast issues at stake, great principles for which to stand, tremendous moral policies that needed evaluating."[14] The first principle and the fundamental condition of membership was loyalty to the institutions of the federal government. In the Club's original bylaws, that conviction was framed this way: "The condition of membership shall be absolute and unqualified loyalty to the government of the United States, and unwavering support of its efforts for the suppression of the Rebellion." With the exception of the last twelve words, that is the Club's rule today. The founders' mission is laid out at greater length and even more intensity in a pamphlet titled *Unconditional Loyalty*, written by Bellows and distributed by the thousands to soldiers in the Union's Army of the Potomac. It ends with this stirring paragraph: "Let our women and children become the propagandists of unconditional loyalty. The country needs not only the fealty of her sons, but of her daughters also. Sing the songs of patriotic devotion at your hearthstones. Let your country have your earliest and your latest prayers. Frown on every syllable of distrust, of wavering, of disrespect, that pollutes the air you breathe. Require of all your friends to be first the friends of the nation! Have nobody's love that does not love the country more! Make a religion of patriotism."[15]

The Founders' New York

As the City's population more than tripled between 1830 and 1860, from 242,000 to 806,000, epidemics were frequent, the streets and sidewalks were unsafe, and decent housing was in short supply even as whole sections of the city—farmland, mansions, estates, and old cemeteries—were ripped apart to make room for cheap buildings. "Other cities are changed chiefly by additions," observed one New York historian. "New York not only adds to itself, but incessantly rends itself in pieces."[16]

Finances ran in a perpetual cycle of boom and bust. When an elderly merchant was asked how many business successes he had seen, he replied mordantly, "The average who have succeeded have been about seven in the hundred. All the rest, ninety-three in the hundred of untold thousands, have been bankrupts."[17] Herman Melville, who knew this world well, observed in his novel *Pierre*, "In our cities families rise and burst like bubbles in a vat." When the Union League Club's founding President, Robert Bowne Minturn was a boy, his father's business failed and he was forced to drop out of school to work as a clerk in a shipping firm. In time, he became a partner, married the senior partner's daughter, and created packet lines running sailing and steam ships to and from Ireland and the market created by the California Gold Rush. One of New York's wealthiest men, Minturn was also one of the most generous, helping to fund Central Park, the Sanitary Commission, and other good causes, even as his own fortunes sometimes depended insecurely on whether a ship reached New York on schedule.

Minturn was a model practitioner of the code of stewardship—a wealthy man personally caring for the underprivileged by establishing a hospital, a shelter, and a nursing service. The code was described by a nineteenth-century New York banker in this description of his partners: "Their ambition was rather to lead simple lives, to attend to their business without ostentation, and to devote a good part of their leisure to the various public, religious, and philanthropic institutions with which they were connected, and to which they gave liberally of their time and money." The banker added, "Character was prized more than wealth, and it brought its great reward in happy, useful lives."[18]

New York historian Iver Bernstein wrote that "Character—moral and personal—was the adhesive that bound together New York's early nineteenth-century commerce and politics."[19] This was the code of the city's Knickerbocker establishment of prosperous old Dutch and Huguenot families who ruled the city for many decades until the rise of the Democratic Party under the brilliant opportunist William M. Tweed.

Not all men of "character" opposed slavery. Too many people grew wealthy from what was sometimes called "the Slave Power." The fact is, the new Club was in the minority in opposing slavery

Robert Bowne Minturn (Club President 1863) took a lead role
in bringing about the construction of Central Park. (Eastman Johnson)

in the City's banks. New York was the largest destination of cotton shipped north and forwarded to England and Europe, and also the largest source of finished goods shipped south. Two generations of New York bankers, factors, and traders grew wealthy off the cotton trade. By one estimate, forty cents of every dollar that Europeans paid for cotton stayed in New York.

The reach of the Slave Power was long and sweeping. At a gathering at the Union League Club toward the end of the Civil War (or as it was commonly known at the Club, "The Great Rebellion"), an elderly member who was a former Congressman and judge, Aaron Vanderpoel, made a dramatic confession. Three decades earlier, in Congress, Vanderpoel had blocked John Quincy Adams from presenting a petition to liberate nine female slaves, ruling that they could not be free because they were not citizens. But in March 1865, in a speech to a crowd of Union League members, the old judge spoke of how much he deeply regretted his prior behavior. One member, George Templeton Strong, took down Vanderpoels's words in his diary: "I tell you that for years before this rebellion, we at the North lived under the tyranny of the slaveholders. I see now that when I was in Congress, almost every important vote I gave was dictated by them and given under the plantation lash. I confess it with shame, and humbly ask pardon of this meeting and of all my fellow-countrymen."[20]

Judge Vanderpoel was an exception as the founding members of the Union League Club opposed slavery. The Club's third President, Charles H. Marshall, was a Nantucket-born Quaker shipmaster who, reportedly, crossed the Atlantic under sail ninety-four times, and was prominent enough to have one of New York's fastest pilot schooners named for him. Marshall came ashore with his social conscience intact to oppose slavery and support the war. After Marshall died in office in 1865, George Templeton Strong noted in his diary that Marshall "upheld the national cause through good report and evil report, even in the dark days."[21]

The first of those "dark days" saw the loss of Fort Sumter in the War's first battle, in April 1861. Minturn, William E. Dodge, and other businessmen responded immediately. They gathered at

and supporting Abraham Lincoln and the Union's war against the Confederacy. New York was financially dependent on the South, and in 1861, 1862, and early 1863, many if not most New Yorkers were cheering the South's victories. True, slaves were no longer sold in New York by the 1850s, though some slave ships continued to be built or be based in the city in defiance of federal and state law. Slave traders, with their nightmarish brutality, may have been chased down, but otherwise much of New York was hospitable to or at least neutral about the fruits of slavery, the most important of which were the bales of cotton piled up on the wharves and in the warehouses of the Hudson and East River, with the proceeds

Daniel Huntington's portrait of Lincoln captures the authority of the man whom Henry W. Bellows called "our great and good President."

New York's pro-Union, pro-Lincoln Republicans made up one of several large political groups in the City. A few Democrats supported the War and were in the first generation of Union League Club members, but most of them favored negotiating a peace with the Confederacy. Republicans considered the War's opponents so dangerous that they nicknamed them after a venomous snake, the copperhead. Their enemies took this as a compliment and responded by cutting out the center of Indian Head copper pennies and wearing the head as a badge on their lapels. The Copperheads were numerous in New York, and they were powerful. "Why, New York was not an American city; it was a foreign city," recalled Joseph H. Choate, the Club's seventh president (1873 to 1876), who was a young man at the time. "It was a Copperhead city. Copperheads sprang up everywhere, and their sentiments mightily prevailed."[23]

"Prevailed" also describes the Confederate Army on the battlefield in the war's initial two years. At the Union League, these fretful times were sometimes considered a trial to be endured in preparation for future happiness. "The glory of the Union League Club is that it was not born of the triumphs of war, but amidst its defeats and despairs," a Club historian, Henry L. Stoddard, would declare at the dinner marking the Club's seventy-fifth anniversary in 1948.[24]

That happy ending was not readily forseeable in 1863—"the dark ages of the City of New York," according to Choate. "The City was divided into two great camps, of which one was maintaining at all hazards the integrity of the Union, and the other was for yielding submissively to the aggressive demands of the State power and even openly siding with the rebels in arms." Choate recalled, "Open demonstrations of treason that were constantly displayed among us."[25]

When Henry Bellows was asked how he responded to the all-too-frequent news of Confederate victories, he replied gloomily, "I read all the imprecatory psalms."[26] Yet in these discouraging times, Bellows, Gibbs, Olmsted, and their friends were quietly forming their new Club.

the New York Chamber of Commerce and, at Dodge's instigation, in ten minutes they raised $21,000 to equip regiments being formed in the City. By May, they had raised more than $100,000. When the hero of the defense of Sumter, Major Robert Anderson, and his troops came to New York, the Republicans put on what was called a "monster rally" in Union Square, with an estimated 100,000 New Yorkers. But Unionists still had to endure bad news from the battlefields and catcalls from the war's opponents.

John Jay

One of the strongest encouraging voices in the formative years was that of Marshall's successor as Club President, John Jay. He refused to hide his convictions behind diplomatic words. In a widely circulated speech, "America Free or America Slave," he said, "Tyranny and treachery, though they may prosper for a while, irresistibly sow the seeds of their own destruction. . . . [L]et us resolve and re-resolve never to falter in our course until we have placed the Federal Government on the side of Freedom."[22]

Words and convictions like those would have qualified John Jay as a Founding Father. In fact, he was a direct descendent of one. When Frederick Law Olmsted was laying out a vision of the Club in his letters to Wolcott Gibbs, he insisted that the membership should represent three groups: men of accomplishment, men of wealth, and "colonial names," by which he meant American aristocrats descended from well-established old families. Jay qualified on all counts. He owned great expanses of land in and outside the City. He was a member of a distinguished old Huguenot family. And not only was his grandfather a Founding Father, the Revolutionary War era diplomat and the first Chief Justice of the Supreme Court of the United States, but his father, William Jay, had founded the American Anti-Slavery Society. The younger John Jay provided legal representation for fugitive slaves, helped found the antislavery Republican Party, and for many years fought to have the Episcopal diocese of New York accept into membership the congregation of the largely African-American St. Philip's Church.

The Club sent President Jay this invitation
to attend a meeting at which
he was honored by the members.
Courtesy of David Mathus.

John Jay was an early and active opponent of slavery. He fearlessly represented runaway slaves who faced recapture under the fugitive slave law. On his 70th birthday, the Club held a dinner in his honor. One friend spoke of his services representing the "Underground Railroad" and how he endured social ostracism and contempt for his ideals. As the Civil War drew to an end, early in 1865, Jay was a member of a Union League Club delegation to Washington to urge Congress to pass the Thirteenth Amendment to the Constitution, abolishing slavery. A year later, he was elected the Club's fourth President (1866 to 1869). Later, he took a leading role in the creation of the Metropolitan Museum of Art, served as Ambassador to Austria, and in 1877 was elected the Club's President again (the only other President to serve twice in the Club's history was another statesman, Elihu Root).

The Sacred Obligation

Following months of discussion about founding a permanent club, on January 15, 1863, Wolcott Gibbs drafted the text for a circular to be distributed to likely members of what he was now calling "the National Club." The political thrust of the document is unmistakable, but even more powerful is the intensity of its convictions. His solemn promise "to enforce a sense of the sacred obligation inherent in citizenship" is as forceful as the Bellows' command, "Make a religion of patriotism." These commitments were far more than the obligations of traditional stewardship, good citizenship, and patriotism. This was an active and energetic engagement with the world for large, vital, and unpopular causes.

Opposite: Robert Bowne Minturn
(President, 1863)
(Launt Thompson, 1866)

33

The Union League Covenant

The urgency of that present great national crisis, and the revolutionary schemes which unprincipled men are plotting to accomplish, make it the immediate duty of all loyal citizens so to organize themselves as to give the most efficient support to the national cause.

It is, therefore, proposed to form in the City of New York a club which may be known as the National Club, the objects of which shall be to cultivate a profound national devotion, as distinguished from that of sectional feeling; to strengthen a love and respect for the Union, and discourage whatever tends to give undue prominence to purely local interests; to discuss and urge upon public attention large and noble schemes of national advancement; to elevate and uphold the popular faith in republican government; to dignify politics as a pursuit and a study; to reawaken a practical interest in public affairs in those who have become discouraged; to enforce a sense of the sacred obligation inherent in citizenship; and, finally, to bring to bear upon the national life all that a body of earnest and patriotic men can accomplish by united effort.

It is believed that an association of such men under a simple organization of a social character, frankly exchanging views upon great questions and actively engaged in disseminating them, could accomplish a noble work. The only requisite for membership, besides unblemished reputation, should be uncompromising and unconditional loyalty to the Nation, and a complete subordination thereto of all other political ideas.

Should these objects meet with your cordial approbation and sympathy, and should you be disposed to take part in the proposed organization, you will please address one of the undersigned at your earliest convenience.

Very respectfully your obedient servants,

Wolcott Gibbs, 59 East 29th Street

George T. Strong, 74 East 21st Street

Henry W. Bellows, 59 East 20th Street

Cornelius R. Agnew, 362 Fifth Avenue

George C. Anthon, 83 East 35th Street

George Gibbs, 261 Greene Street

George F. Allen, 42 East 24th Street

William J. Hoppin, 61 Pine Street[27]

There was some disagreement concerning the meaning of a phrase at the opening of the third paragraph: "A simple organization of a social character." How simple? How social? The answers would disappoint Gibbs and Olmsted, who wanted it to be a purely political organization, with no clubhouse or other facilities to compromise its ideals with pleasantries. Many men who generally shared the two men's aims favored making the new organization something more of a social club, like the three existing clubs in the city at the time, with which many prospective members were familiar. What

resulted was, in the words of a later member, Theodore Roosevelt, Jr., a club that had a blended "politico-social" character.[28]

Soon "The National Club" was replaced by a name that already had national significance. A loosely organized body called variously "The Union League" and "The Loyal League" was springing up across the Union states in opposition to pro-South, anti-war politicians. Although the Union League of New York was the first substantial club with this name to be conceived, the first one to actually be organized and incorporated with the name Union

North Union Square, Taken 1868
(Richard J. Murphy)
The Union League Club made its first home in the second building from the left, located near Union Square.

William J. Hoppin (Club President 1871-72) helped William Cullen Bryant
and other members found the Metropolitan Museum of Art.
(Franklin Tuttle)

Dr. Cornelius R. Agnew, a medical advisor to the U.S. Sanitary Commission,
signed the Union League Covenant.
(Eastman Johnson)

League was in Philadelphia. Bellows said this was just; if the country's formative document, the Declaration of Independence, came out of Philadelphia, so should this transformative institution of American freedom.

The Clubs of New York
The new club was a different type of organization than the city's three leading clubs in 1863: the Union Club, the New York Yacht Club, and the Century Association. The Union Club, New York's oldest elite club, was founded in 1836 as a social center for a group that Mayor Philip Hone, in his diary, described as "a number of our most distinguished citizens."[29] Many of these men came from patrician Dutch and Huguenot Knickerbocker families that had dominated the city's business, political, and social life for decades.

One aspect of the Union Club that some of its members disliked was its tolerance of slave-holding Southerners, some of whom were members. After the first shots were fired in the Civil War, an incident arose involving rebel Attorney General, and later

Charles King, President of Columbia College, defended the Union cause.
His home was attacked during the Draft Riots. (A. Wenzler)

The Griffin

Judging by the behavior of George Templeton Strong, the founders must have been in a high state of exuberance after signing their organizational document. Normally a cautious man who reserved his sharp opinions for his diary, on the day after the charter was signed Strong made a special trip to the Century Association, where he was a member, with the sole purpose of publicly snubbing Copperheads, or (as he wrote in his diary) "showing a cold shoulder to two or three of its habitués who secessionize."[31] This was not a whim. Strong and the other founders believed they were defending not only the physical Union but also the higher principle of supporting the established order of legal institutions against radicals, rabble-rousers, crooked politicians, and anarchists of all stripes, whether their names were Jefferson Davis or William M. Tweed. An excellent example of their aversion to extremes is the title of an address to the members, which the Club published and distributed widely: "Revolution against Free Government Not a Right but a Crime."

These convictions were expressed in the founders' choice of the symbol for the Union League Club. It was the griffin, the heraldic image of a majestic half-lion, half-eagle that guards priceless possessions. Decades later, this magnificent representation was replaced by another, the eagle, the symbol of American liberty.

Secretary of War, Judah P. Benjamin. The episode is described in some detail in the Union League Club member Le Grand B. Cannon's Civil War memoir, *Personal Remembrances of the Rebellion, 1861-1866*, which was published in 1895.

A review of the two clubs' membership rolls in the 1860s and seventies shows that while some men were members of both clubs, the overlap is sparse among the Union League Club's leaders. Of the eight signers of the Club's January 15, 1863 circular, only one, William J. Hoppin, was a Union Club member. Of the seven

Thanksgiving Turkeys

The main cause, of course, was the Union, which in the Club's first three years usually meant the Union Army. The founders looked out for the welfare of the troops in many ways. One year the Sanitary Commission donated cartloads of clothing, including 1,255 flannel shirts and 892 handkerchiefs. After President Lincoln established Thanksgiving Day in 1864, Union League Club member George W. Blunt, who kept a ship's chandlery near South Street, proposed that the Club help soldiers celebrate properly by providing them with turkeys and all the trimmings. Theodore Roosevelt, Senior, (the father of the President) volunteered to serve as treasurer of this enterprise, and within three weeks he had arranged for the donation of thousands of turkeys totaling some 80,000 pounds of poultry. The twenty-six-page list of donors includes the names of many wealthy New Yorkers, and also of indigent ones, such as "poor woman, four ducks," and "Mrs. Bergen, four mince pies." The Club shipped it all to three Union armies in the field. A fourth army, that of General William T. Sherman, could not be located because it was on its fast march to the sea. Sherman eventually wrote in to say that he would be pleased to send some southern turkeys to New York. The cost to the Club and its members was slightly under $57,000, the equivalent of $785,000 today.

The gift of turkeys to the military became a tradition at the Union League Club that is still carried on in donations of turkeys to the Soldiers', Sailors', Marines', Coast Guards', and Airmen's Club on Lexington Avenue in New York City.

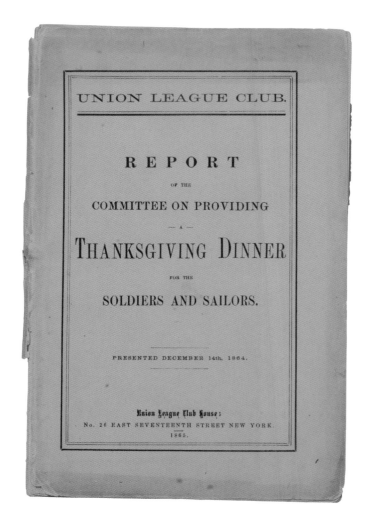

UNION LEAGUE CLUB.

REPORT

OF THE

COMMITTEE ON PROVIDING

— A —

THANKSGIVING DINNER

FOR THE

SOLDIERS AND SAILORS.

PRESENTED DECEMBER 14th, 1864.

Union League Club House:
No. 26 EAST SEVENTEENTH STREET NEW YORK.
1865.

Presidents elected in the Club's first decade, only two (Hoppin and Charles H. Marshall) also belonged to the older club. None of the Union League Club's cultural leaders—including the poet and editor William Cullen Bryant and the newspaper publishers Horace Greeley and George Jones—were Union Club members.

The New York Yacht Club was formed in 1844 by a collection of Knickerbockers and newcomers who enjoyed the new pastime of yachting, or pleasure sailing. Despite its name, the Yacht Club had its clubhouse across the Hudson at Hoboken, New Jersey, on property owned by the family of the founding Commodore, John Cox Stevens. Seven years later, Stevens and several friends built a schooner, *America*, and sent her to England, where she beat the English at their own game in their home waters. The trophy they won came to be called the "America's Cup". Eventually, the Yacht Club was tainted by the Slave Power. In 1858, one of its members was discovered to be the owner of a slave ship that carried more than 400 slaves from the Congo to Georgia. The New York Yacht Club expelled the owner from membership and banned its members from ever mentioning his name or the name of the ship again.

The New York Club with which the Union League Club had the closest relationship was the Century Association, formed in 1847 for men with interests in literature, the fine arts, and culture. The Century was also controversial among Unionists. Many of its members were Southern sympathizers, foremost among them the Club's first President, Gulian Crommelin Verplanck, an elderly writer and political figure of Dutch heritage who was so voluble a Copperhead that he was deposed from office.

Three weeks after Gibbs' circular was signed and distributed, on February 6, eight men gathered in the headquarters of the Sanitary Commission, at 823 Broadway near Eleventh Street, to sign a document organizing the Club. Here is how the mission and purpose were described:

The condition of membership shall be absolute and unqualified loyalty to the government of the United States, and unwavering support of its efforts for the suppression of the Rebellion.

The primary object of the Association shall be to discountenance and rebuke by moral and social influences, all disloyalty to the Federal Government, and to that end the members will use every proper means in public and private.

We pledge ourselves by every means in our power, collectively and individually, to resist to the uttermost every attempt against the territorial Integrity of the nation.[30]

The signers (in the order of their names) were: Wolcott Gibbs, George Templeton Strong, Henry W. Bellows, Cornelius R. Agnew, George C. Anthon, George Gibbs, George F. Allen, and William J. Hoppin.

Most of the eight, including Agnew, a doctor, were active in the Sanitary Commission. Frederick Law Olmsted would have added to their number had he come up to New York from the Commission's field office in Washington. Paradoxically, the Club's two progenitors, Wolcott Gibbs and Frederick Law Olmsted, left New York just as their idea was coming into fruition. Gibbs moved to Cambridge, Massachusetts, where he became a Harvard professor. Olmsted, exhausted after two years of work for the Commission, went to California, where he managed a silver mine. He returned to New York and joined the Club before eventually resettling in Massachusetts, where he continued his great and influential career as a landscape architect.

For all Strong's exuberance, a month after the organizing document was signed the movement seemed frozen in place, unsure of its structure and purpose. There was a tension between the pure political views of Gibbs and Olmsted, and a feeling on the part of others that this should be, at least in part, a social club, with a proper clubhouse. "We are sticking in the mud, foundering among divers theories of what we out to be: clubhouse or mere association?" Strong asked himself in his diary. He was optimistic: "After we have passed a certain point and settled these and other questions finally, no matter which way, we shall begin to develop fast."[32] Three days after Strong wrote that glum note, Robert B. Minturn and another successful "merchant prince," George Griswold, stepped up and took charge. Strong recorded the results of that meeting in his diary: "We made considerable headway last night; raised annual dues from $10 to $25, and gravitated toward the clubhouse plan, on which alone we can accomplish anything."[33] Minturn was elected as the Club's first President. The Vice Presidents included a number of merchants and other businessmen, including Moses Taylor, founder of a predecessor of Citibank; the department store magnate Alexander T. Stewart; James W. Beekman of Beekman Place; William H. Aspinwall, whose railroad across the isthmus of Panama carried people to the Gold Rush; and David Hoadley, a pioneer in South American trade. Clearly desiring diversity of backgrounds and professions (so long as the members agreed with the founding principles), the Club would elect other Vice Presidents from a range of backgrounds, including the irrepressible idealist Henry W. Bellows, the historian George Bancroft (who was elected President of the Century Association in 1864), and the banker Jesse Seligman and two of his brothers, who were members of one of New York's most prominent Jewish families. The membership also included some of the City's most important cultural figures, among them William Cullen Bryant, President Charles King of Columbia College, and the painter John Frederick Kensett, one of many important artists who were members and whose works have graced the Club's walls.

By the summer of 1863 the Club had 350 members and a small, leased Clubhouse overlooking Union Square. The membership grew so rapidly, reaching 833 at the end of 1865, that the Club capped resident membership at 1,000. In 1870, the total of 1,005 resident members and 385 non-residents made the Union League Club the largest club in New York.

William E. Dodge, Jr., one of the Club's "merchant princes," took the lead in many of the efforts to support the Union. Soon after the surrender of Fort Sumter, he helped organize a massive pro-war rally of tens of thousands of New Yorkers at Union Square. Later, he worked with Columbia College President Charles King and other Union League Club members to help run the Loyal Publication Society, which published more than ninety pro-Union pamphlets. The Club also provided financial support to other Unionist periodicals, such as the *Nation* and *Harper's Weekly*.

As troops were recruited, Dodge and Theodore Roosevelt, Sr., developed a pioneering allotment system that sent a portion of soldiers' pay home to their wives and other relatives. When Roosevelt learned that the policy was extremely unpopular among the troops, who saw it only as taking cash from their pockets, he dutifully went out in the field and visited sixty New York regiments to make the case that anything that was good for a soldier's family is good for a soldier. Whether he made many converts is not known, but the allotment system remained in force. When Roosevelt learned that the war's interruption of cotton shipments to England had caused many mill workers to lose their jobs, he, Dodge, Minturn, and New York City Mayor George Opdyke organized a relief committee that sent seven shiploads of cash, food, and goods to mill towns. At the same time, Opdyke and the newspaper publisher Horace Greeley arranged for relief shipments to Ireland.[34]

These were men of principle. A writer, diplomat, and Club member named Henry Bergh was on his way home from an assignment in Russia when he stopped in England and visited the founder of the Royal Society for the Prevention of Cruelty to Animals. Bergh came home and founded the American Society for the Prevention of Cruelty to Animals. As for William E. Dodge, Jr., he was a dedicated Temperance man who eventually quit the Union League Club because it had a bar. No matter how much he agreed with its other concerns, this was the one that counted most to him.

John Brown, framed with a lock of John Brown's hair obtained at his Funeral in North Elba, New York by Joel B. Erhardt
and a portion of the original notes of Wendell Phillips from which he delivered his oration on that occasion.

The Union League Club, 1863–2013

The Union League in the Civil War

Less than five months after it was founded, the Union League Club was caught up in a crisis that swept through the City. The Draft Riots were the crucible for one of the Club's best-known and widely admired initiatives—the creation of three Union Army regiments staffed mainly by black soldiers.

During the winter of 1863, short-term enlistments of the first large group of army volunteers expired at the same time as enthusiasm for the war bottomed out in the North. New York City alone was short nearly 19,000 volunteers. With recruiters unable to fill the ranks, in July, the federal government began to conscript soldiers using a lottery system. Anyone who was selected could exempt himself either by paying a commutation fee of $300, which covered only the current draft call (another fee might have to be paid in the future), or by finding a substitute and negotiating a bounty that might run as high as $1,000. When the first draft lottery in the City was held on July 11, 1863, many middle class and wealthy New Yorkers arranged for substitutes. Among them were future Union League Club member J. Pierpont Morgan and founding member Theodore Roosevelt, Sr., who supported the war as a matter of principle, but declined to fight because he was married to a native of Georgia who sympathized with the Confederacy. At a time when a man earning $1,000 a year was doing exceptionally well—and when approximately one out of every ten men of draft age died in the war—this system outraged working people. William M. Tweed, then on the rise, saw an opportunity and paid the fee or bounty for men in exchange for political loyalty.

Opposite: *Presentation of the Colors by the Ladies of New York to the 20th Regiment* (E. L. Henry, 1869)

Lincoln and His Cabinet

Sketches of members of Lincoln's Cabinet were made by artist Frank Bicknell Carpenter for the well-known group portrait on the facing page. The sketches and a copy of *Lincoln and His Cabinet Assembled to Sign the Emancipation Proclamation* are in the Club's collection.

IMAGES THIS PAGE:
(Clockwise from upper right)
Salmon P. Chase, Secretary of the Treasury; Edward Bates, Attorney General; Edwin M. Stanton, Secretary of War

IMAGES THIS PAGE:
(Above, left to right)
Gideon Welles, Secretary of
the Navy; William H. Seward,
Secretary of State; Montgomery
Blair, Postmaster General;
*Lincoln and His Cabinet
Assembled to Sign the
Emancipation Proclamation*
(Frank Bicknell Carpenter)

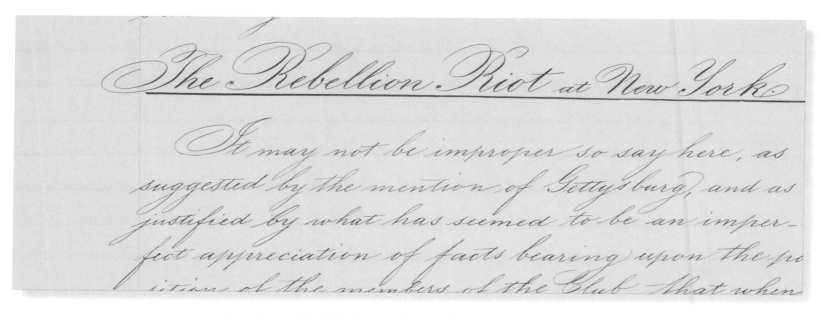

The Rebellion Riot at New York

It may not be improper so say here, as suggested by the mention of Gettysburg, and as justified by what has seemed to be an imperfect appreciation of facts bearing upon the po... ition of the members of the Club that when

Copy of a page of the ULC minute book detailing efforts to combat the Draft Riots.

Two days after the lottery, the grumbling became violence. The story of the Draft Riots is clouded in legends laid down long ago. Thousands of men and women flooded the streets in protest. Some protests were spontaneous and others were led by or involved the City's gangs—some Irish, some anti-immigrant—with strange names like the Dead Rabbits, Bowery Boys, Shirt Tails, and True Blue Americans.

The Draft Riots ranged across the metropolitan area and even into Westchester County, where John Jay was personally threatened by Copperheads. Estimates of the total mortality in the riots exceeded 1,000. All New Yorkers suffered, but the City's black citizens suffered most. African-American homes and churches were burned to the ground, as was the Colored Orphan Asylum at Fifth Avenue and Forty-Fourth Street, and at least 100 African Americans died, including an estimated eighteen by lynching. "They are the most peaceable, sober, and inoffensive of our poor," George Templeton Strong sympathetically wrote of New York's African Americans in his diary. Comparing the assaults with anti-Semitic riots in the Middle Ages, Strong growled, "This is a nice town to call itself a centre of civilized life!"[35] Walt Whitman characterized the violence as "the devil's own work"—words so appropriate for this part race war, part class war that historian Barnet Schecter chose them for the title of his recent history of the Draft Riots.[36]

Another target was the Union League Club, which was identified with the war and the draft system. Mobs attacked the homes of Union League Club members, including Columbia College President Charles King and Horace Greeley, editor of the *New York Tribune*. One mob laid siege to the Clubhouse, where members rushed to barricade the doors and posted sentries with rifles in the windows. Elsewhere, Club member Leonard Jerome helped defend the offices of *The New York Times* by manning a Gatling gun.[37] Amid broad fear that a radical revolution was imminent, the Club's officers pressed the city, state, and federal governments to suppress the riots through "an immediate and terrible" display of military force.[38] William E. Dodge, Jr. was preparing to raise a volunteer company when Major David Hoadley, a Union League

When this portrait was rendered by Emanuel Leutze, William H. Seward
was not a wartime Cabinet member, but a Presidential candidate opposing Lincoln.
(Emanuel Leutze)

Daniel Webster
(Albert Gallatin Hoit)
The artist captured Daniel Webster's powerful personality.

Vice President, and other Club members who had helped win the battle of Gettysburg under General William Scott Hancock raced to the City. When Police Superintendent John A. Kennedy, a Union League Club member, was seriously injured in a riot on the first day, another Club member, Commissioner Thomas Acton, took charge of the police and reportedly did not sleep until order was restored. The Union League Club would elect Acton one of its first Honorary Life Members.[39]

Joseph H. Choate (later the Union League Club President from 1873 to 1876) rescued a black family from their home as a mob was breaking through the windows with pick axes. Responding to an initiative by Union League members Jonathan Sturges (another future Club President) and Henry J. Raymond, editor of *The New York Times*, a Committee of Merchants for the Relief of Colored People was established and raised almost $40,000 (the equivalent today of more than $500,000) and distributed the funds to 2,500

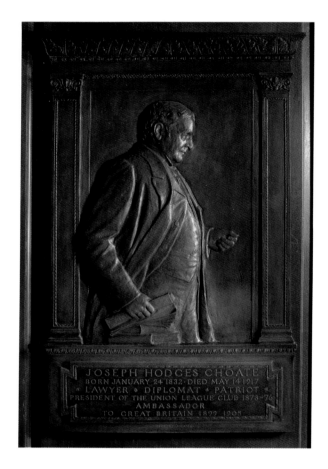

Joseph H. Choate (Club President 1873-76) defended a black family during the Draft Riots. This bronze portrait is in the Clubhouse foyer. (Herbert Adams)

displaced or injured African Americans.

Another philanthropic effort headed by a Club member was a fund for the families of the policemen and the firemen (all volunteers) killed or injured during the Draft Riots. Founded by Union League member George Jones, publisher of the *Times*, with the assistance of Club member Leonard Jerome, the Riot Relief Fund raised and distributed $23,000 in a week. The fund still exists and helps the families of deceased firefighters, police officers, and members of the National Guard. Afterwards, State Senator and

Union League Club co-founder William Laimbeer overcame the opposition of Tammany Hall and Boss Tweed and pushed through the state legislature a bill providing for a paid, professional New York Fire Department.

"Our Club's First Work"

In the wake of the Draft Riots, in November 1863, the Union League formed a Committee on Volunteering to support service in the war. Two of the committee's members, a Van Rensselaer and a Roosevelt, were from distinguished Knickerbocker families. Another, Jackson H. Schultz, was a leather merchant and a founder of the city's most combative reform organization, the Committee of Seventy. Two committee members had served in the military: George Bliss, Jr., a captain in a New York artillery regiment, and Le Grand B. Cannon, a banker and abolitionist who, as a Union Army officer, had protected runaway slaves, called "contrabands," from Southern agents.

While many Club members served, the committee did not call on the Club's members to join the army. Rather, it requested them to donate funds to induce other men to sign up and join a regiment. "We feel that every member should have at least one man fighting for him in the armies of the Union, and that a small additional bounty will accomplish this result," the committee told the members.[40] The Club resolved to found regiments of black soldiers. The first "colored" regiment in the war was the Fifty-Fourth Massachusetts Infantry, formed in February 1863.

The Fifty-Fourth's heroism and sacrifice at Fort Wagner, South Carolina, inspired many northern African Americans to demand that they, too, be allowed to fight against slavery. As "colored" regiments were formed in many states (but not New York), the percentage of black men who volunteered for military service tended to exceed that of eligible whites. Several regiments were integrated but many more were all-black in the ranks of enlisted men, with white officers.

According to Cannon, the Club had two reasons to organize a "colored regiment": it would raise New York's black residents

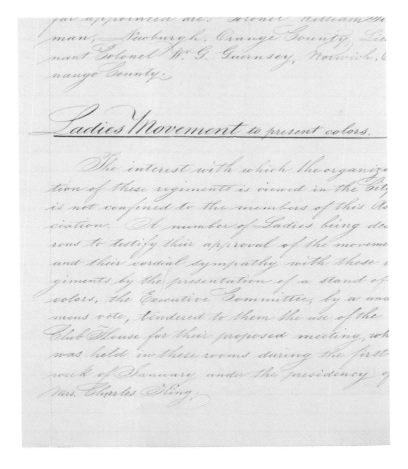

The topic of this excerpt from the Club minutes is the presentation of colors by the ladies to the 20th Colored Regiment in March 1863.

act of the Club is more memorable than the raising of the three regiments of United States Colored Troops."[41]

A committee headed by Bliss raised funds as recruiters fanned out across the state. "Men of Color to Arms! To Arms!" read one recruiting poster, echoing a famous cry of reformer Frederick Douglass. The regiment's 1,000 enlisted men, all African Americans recruited from Long Island, Brooklyn, Manhattan, and upstate New York, trained on Riker's Island. When the commanding officer, Colonel Nelson B. Bartram, was asked if his black troops were prepared to march through hostile City streets to the wharf, he reportedly replied, "Give me room to land my regiment, and if it cannot march through New York, it is not fit to go into the field."[42] Racial tension ran so high that two all-white marching bands refused the Club's offer to participate in the parade before a third finally agreed.

On March 5, 1864, the Twentieth Regiment (following Superintendent of Police Kennedy) marched to the Union League's Clubhouse on Seventeenth Street, where nearly 100 mothers, wives, sisters, and daughters of members (headed by a Southerner, Mrs. John Jacob Astor) presented the regiment's colors to the soldiers and officers. George Templeton Strong described the sight of this parade as "among the most solemn memories of my life thus far." A newspaper reported, "A vast crowd of citizens of every shade of color, every phase of social and political life, filled the square and streets, and every door, window, veranda, tree, and house-top that commanded a view of the scene was peopled with spectators." The *Times* juxtaposed this spectacular ceremony against the ignominious Draft Riots: "Eight months ago, the African race in this City were literally hunted down like wild beasts. How astonishingly has all this been changed! The same men who could not have shown themselves in the most obscure street in the City without perils of instant death, even though in the most suppliant attitude, now march in solid platoons with shouldered muskets."

In the main address to the regiment, which stood at attention in front of the Union League Clubhouse, Charles King told the soldiers, "When you put on the uniform and swear allegiance to

"from their degradation" by allowing them to serve their country, and it would purge the City of "the taint of that wicked, infamous, and inhuman riot" of the summer of 1863. Soon there were sufficient funds to create three regiments of black soldiers, commanded by white officers. After Governor Horatio Seymour refused to approve an integrated regiment for the New York State militia, the Club arranged with the Lincoln administration to federalize three black regiments, which became the Twentieth, Twenty-Sixth, and Thirty-First United States Colored Troops. Cannon would say that of all the Club's achievements in its first quarter century, "no

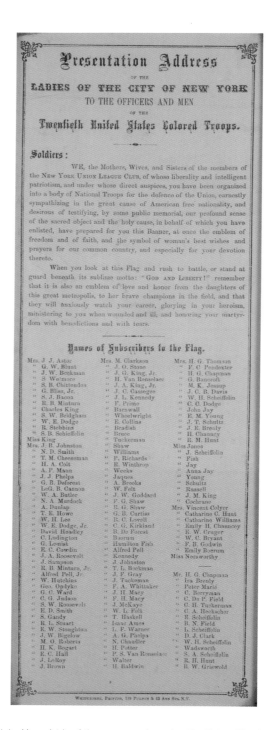

Original broadside of the ceremony honoring the Colored Regiment.

the standard of the Union, you stand emancipated, regenerated, and disenthralled—the peer of the proudest soldier in the land."[43] The men of the Twentieth then marched to the waterfront and boarded a ship headed South. They fought in the Battle for Port Hudson, in Louisiana, but otherwise were assigned to non-combat, support duties in Texas, Florida, and Tennessee before the regiment was disbanded in October 1865. The regiment's losses totaled 275 men. The Twenty-Sixth Colored Regiment served in South Carolina, losing 145 men. The Club's third black regiment, the Thirty-First, was merged with another regiment, saw action in the Battle of Richmond, and was billeted at Appomattox Court House, blocking the retreat of Lee's army.

Many veterans of the Union League's black regiments remained in the South, but a number of them returned north. At least six are buried at the Evergreens Cemetery, in Brooklyn, in a lot reserved for a post of the Grand Army of the Republic, the organization of former Union Army soldiers. These and the other black soldiers who served in the war (a number approaching 180,000) are honored at the African American Civil War Memorial and Museum, in Washington, D.C.[44]

Among the Union League Club's accomplishments, raising the regiments are the most honored by its members. For decades, the Club's *Yearbook* (called the "Blue Book") has included a one-page history of the Club's Civil War Colored Regiments under the headline "Our Club's First Work."

Election and Tragedy

None of this ensured Lincoln's re-election in 1864. The Democratic candidate was former Union Army General, George McClellan, who had moved to New York after Lincoln had relieved him of command. A French visitor to the City in the fall of 1864, Ernest Duvergier de Hauranne, was astonished by the viciousness of the Presidential campaign, particularly in New York. "There is truly nothing less worthy of respect than the people of New York when aroused by political emotion," he wrote home. "Everything was well-seasoned with blasphemy." [45]

Robert Gould Shaw was not the only white officer of a black regiment.
The Union League Club formed three "colored" regiments. (Giuseppe Fagnani)

which it is the object of the Club to con
upon the country, before discussing the
...forts and conveniences which it proposes at
same time to secure to its members.

Committee on Volunteers.

On the 12th of ——— November, on the
...mendation of the Executive Committee,
after careful consideration, the Club ap-
...ed a Committee of seven members, with...

...The Club appointed, as such commi...
Messrs. Van Rensselaer, Cannon, Bacon,
...A. Roosevelt, Kirkland, Cowdin and
Bliss.

Organization of colored Regiments
...The Committee, finding that other agenci...

Engaging with the great issues of the day, the Board of Directors discussed reports
from the Committees on Volunteers and Organization of Colored Regiments.

Rumors and reports that the Confederacy was collapsing and in disarray reached New York in March 1865. Every night, the Union League Clubhouse, off Union Square, was packed with members reading telegraphed reports. When word came on April 3rd that General Grant had taken Petersburg, George Templeton Strong sprinted down to Trinity Church and persuaded the sexton to ring the church bells. The streets filled with throngs who sang lengthy choruses of psalms, hymns, and patriotic anthems, and when they reached the end of "The Star Spangled Banner" they repeated the last line, "The Land of the Free, and the Home of the Brave," over

and over in a great chorus. "It seemed a revelation of profound national feeling," Strong wrote in his diary. "Men embraced and hugged each other, kissed each other, retreated into doorways to dry their eyes and come out again to flourish their hats and hurrah." Making his way uptown to the Union League's Clubhouse, Strong joined a crowd of members who were presenting speeches and reciting war memories amid dense noise from the streets: fireworks, hurrahing, and performances of the psalms, *Te Deums*, and Beethoven symphonies. "There will be many sore throats in New York tomorrow," Strong wrote in his diary. "It seems like a Fourth

Union Army Generals in the Collection

President Ulysses S. Grant
(Enoch Wood Perry)

Philip Sheridan
(Giuseppe Fagnani)

President Ulysses S. Grant and Philip Sheridan were among many Army and Navy officers honored at the Club.

Clockwise from above:
General William T. Sherman (Chester Harding);
General George Thomas (Eastman Johnson);
General George C. Meade (Thomas Hicks)

"I Esteem the Union League Club"

In December 1889, General William Tecumseh Sherman sent the Club a check for $5 for a ticket to a reception for South American diplomats who were attending a conference in the City. Club Secretary Sigourney W. Fay promptly returned the check with a note saying that of all the men who should be an honored guest at the reception, it should be General Sherman, "who did all he could to save the United States of America from going to pieces, and who today is the best beloved of all her citizens."

Sherman replied: "I esteem The Union League Club of New York so highly that I feel duty bound in some way to reciprocate the very many favors I have experienced."

of July night—such a fusillade and cannonade is going on. Thus ends a day *sui generis* in my life."[46]

Then came the devastating news of Lincoln's assassination. Strong and Henry W. Bellows attended the funeral, and the Club was given a place of honor when the train bearing Lincoln's body arrived in New York, where the Union League organized a massive memorial service at Union Square. Union League Club members subsequently commissioned a towering bronze statue of Lincoln by Henry Kirke Brown. It was placed it the south end of Union Square in 1869 with an inscription, "The Statue of Lincoln was sponsored by the Union League Club, a Republican Organization."[47] In 2010, the History Committee restored and installed a new plaque for the statue, which is now at the north end of the park.

George Templeton Strong spent some time going through the Club's dozens of scrapbooks of the war that had been assembled by a member, Thomas Seaman Townsend. Although the events described in these clippings were recent, Strong found himself in a quandary trying to make sense of them. "It seemed like reading the records of some remote age and of a people wholly unlike our own," he wrote in his diary. "So many notions were then put forward as axioms which are now seen to have been preposterous."[48] The Club hosted many celebrations of the victory, and welcomed as honored guests the heroes of the war, including Generals Grant, Sherman, Warren, and Burnside, and Admirals and Commodores Farragut, du Pont, Rogers, Winslow, and Cushing. Soon after Farragut's victory at the battle of Mobile Bay, Union League members Theodore Roosevelt, Sr., Henry L. Pierson, and Frank E. Howe sent him a fine bejeweled sword inscribed with the words, "Presented to Rear Admiral David G. Farragut by Members of the Union League Club, as a token of their appreciation of his gallant Services rendered in defense of his Country. New York. April 23rd 1864." This sword is now on display at the Smithsonian Institution.

But for most members the most satisfying visit was the one from Vice-President Schuyler Colfax, who assured the members that President Lincoln had often leaned on the Union League Club.

An Internal Battle

The war was over, but strong feelings remained. When Copperheads who had long scorned the Club began applying for membership, Strong (the chairman of the Admissions Committee) sardonically commented in his diary, "We are discovering now with some surprise that everybody . . . has been an 'uncompromising Union man from the first.' What a pity we had not known this a year ago; we should have been saved much uneasiness." He took some satisfaction in leading the Committee on Admissions in turning down "half a score" of Copperheads.[49]

Other members worked to secure jobs for veterans. Some established a service called the Soldiers Messenger Corps that stationed wounded veterans in parts of Manhattan to deliver letters. One issue left undecided by the surrender at Appomattox was how to treat the South. While many Republicans were radical Reconstructionists who favored punitive treatment of the former rebels, others made efforts to try to bring about national reunion, North with South. Future Club President Chauncey M. Depew (1886 to 1892) helped create the American Plant and Loan Company to make loans to Southern cotton growers and sugar planters to enable them to get their products to market.

The fate of the President of the Confederacy was up in the air. "A rather lively theoretical controversy has arisen of and concerning Jeff Davis," Strong reflected the day the news came of Lee's surrender. "Shall we hang him, when and if we catch him, or shall we let him run?" Strong privately opted for a public lynching.[50] Lincoln was reported to be more generous, but when he died, the full power of retribution was unleashed.

The Club's Committee on Political Reform was a vocal, nationally known thorn in the side of corruption and complacency. Its main targets were, at the national level, politicians attempting to end Reconstruction and, locally, agents of political corruption. The committee's investigations and printed reports (many of which were reported in the newspapers) attacked an astonishing range of topics. All lay safely outside the Club's walls until May 1867, when founding member Horace Greeley—editor of one of the country's most influential newspapers, a loud voice of opposition against the Slave Power and political corruption—shocked the country by helping to bail Jefferson Davis out of prison. Greeley had always been something of a wild card, but this was too much for his fellow members of the Union League Club. He vigorously defended himself, saying that the time for retribution must end for the sake of national reunion. That did not appease some of his outraged fellow members at the Union League Club, who demanded that the Club call Greeley to account at a special meeting. If the members there were not satisfied with his defense, he would be expelled.

Greeley would have none of it. He replied in an editorial in the *Tribune*, "I do not recognize you as capable of judging or even fully apprehending me. You evidently regard me as a weak sentimentalist, mislead by maudlin philosophy. I arraign you as narrow-minded blockheads."[51] The members met without him and, after a lengthy, bitter debate, rejected motions to punish him. Greeley remained a gadfly. He supported the Club's campaign against Tweed, yet ran for President on an independent ticket in 1872. Pilloried by his former allies, many of them Union League Club members, Greeley lost badly and died soon afterwards. At his funeral, a large delegation of Club members marched behind his bier down Fifth Avenue.

Bellows blamed the nasty divorce between the Union League and one of its most gifted members in large part on residual bitterness from the war. "Toleration of a civil sort was extinct during the rebellion and long after." But he also accused the Club of intolerance. "No club can exist and flourish in such times which does not maintain and exhibit the most careful respect for the individual opinions of all honest men."[52]

As intense and controversial as the early years in the Club's history were, their memory was treasured by the founders. Not long before his death in 1894, John Jay wrote a brief summary of the Union League's first years in the midst of the Civil War:

"In New York, where mob law had prevailed, the Union League Club upheld the loyalty of the city, the credit of the nation, and the Sanitary Commission; raised troops for Hancock in addition to its own colored regiments; stimulated the ardour of our soldiers and the patriotism of our country; welcomed, of the army, Grant and Sherman, Warren and Burnside, and of the navy, Farragut, du Pont, and Rogers, Winslow and the youthful Cushing; verifying in its spirit and action the remark of Vice-President Colfax that on the Union League Club Lincoln had leaned in the darkest hours."[53]

Art Gallery

The Union League Club
of New York

~~~~~

SEVENTY-FIFTH
ANNIVERSARY
RECEPTION AND EXHIBITION

February 6, 1938
4-6 P.M.

~~~~~

The PRESIDENT and OFFICERS of the Club will receive in the LOUNGE on the First Floor.

REFRESHMENTS will be served in the MAIN DINING ROOM, Third Floor, and in the GREAT HALL, Second Floor.

MEMBERS and GUESTS are invited to view the PAINT-INGS and ART OBJECTS which are listed in this pamphlet.

Program for 75th Anniversary Dinner and Art Exhibition

A Memory of the Mountains
(Joseph Jefferson, 1897)

In the Woods
(George Hetzel, 1878)

Near Trumbull, Connecticut
(Richard William Hubbard, 1875)

John F. Kensett's Islands
(Peter Layne Arguimbau, 1987)

Last Reflections ("Twilight over Plum Island and the Parker River")
(Charles Harold Davis)

Pond in Rhode Island
(Robert Ward Van Boskerck)

The Kearsarge and the Alabama
(Henri Durand-Brager, 1869)

Newport Rocks
(Casimir Clayton Griswold, 1869)

Prairie Sunset
(Alexander H. Wyant, 1868)

Housatonic Valley
(Alexander H. Wyant)

At the Inn
(Frank D. Millet, 1884)

Landscape with River
(Edward B. Gay, 1868)

Sailing in Moonlight
(Edward Moran)

Landscape with River
(Richard William Hubbard, 1868)

Mediterranean Scene
(Samuel Colman, 1867)

Young Woman Reading a Book
(W. V. Birney)

Peter Cooper
(J. Alden Weir, 1883)

George Washington
(Anonymous, style of Gilbert)

Medals honoring centennial of victory in the American Revolution (1883)

Saranac Lake
(Homer Dodge Martin)

A Summer Morning, Star Island
(Arthur Quartley)

The Jungfrau
(A. Jenny, 1868)

Landscape with Sheep
(William H. Lippincott)

Mercury Bronze
donated to the Club in memory of Ernest Yale Gallaher

Providing for Her Cubs
(August Nicolas Cain, 1866)

Ships of the Plains
(Samuel Colman)

Blanket Pony Strategy
(Frederick Remington, 1902)

JOHN JAY
Grandson of a Founding
Father, abolitionist, diplomat,
and two-time Club President,
he stimulated creation of the
Metropolitan Museum of Art.

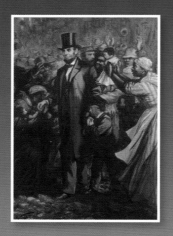

DOOMED BY CARTOON
Acclaimed cartoonist, artist,
and member Thomas Nast
portrays the deep affection
felt by freed slaves
for Abraham Lincoln.

ARTIST MEMBERS
With Eastman Johnson, Daniel
Huntington, and other famous
painters in its membership,
the Club develops a magnificent
collection of American art.

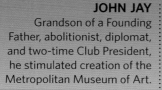

1870

1873

1875

Part Two

The Gilded Age

A NEW CLUBHOUSE
After renting quarters for years, the Club builds the first of its two elegant clubhouses. "No more notable building exists on Fifth Avenue."

LADY LIBERTY
The Club leads the American effort to build the Statue of Liberty and Grant's Tomb, which are unveiled in stirring ceremonies.

CLUB LIFE
The Club's activities continue to include politics. The members also play billiards and cards, and offer hospitality to military officers during the Spanish-American War.

MEMBERS GATHER
Tradition and ceremony rule at the monthly meetings. A hand bell calls members up the staircase, and great issues are debated. The meetings end with all singing "America."

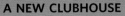

1881   1886 & 1897   1898   1900

Artists, Boss Tweed, and Lady Liberty

After Appomattox, the members' concerns broadened into new areas that were by turn cultural, political, and patriotic. One of the first initiatives was the creation of the Metropolitan Museum of Art.

Before the museum opened in 1870, most art exhibits in the City were held in the galleries of the Union League Club and the Century Association, or at fundraising events. Several Union League Club members collected paintings and sculpture mostly by European or English artists, with some new interest in American artists. One of the most ambitious of these collectors was a Club founding member, Jonathan Sturges. The father of J. Pierpont Morgan's first wife, Sturges was a member of a group of amateur artists called the Sketch Club, out of which the Century Association was founded. Sturges collected European masters and also the work of Frederick Church and other American artists in the Hudson River School.

Opposite: *Their Pride*
(Thomas Hovenden, 1888)

After his election as the Club's second President in 1864, when Robert Minturn moved to Europe, Sturges introduced the Club's policy of acquiring American art and admitting artist members by accepting paintings in lieu of dues. In April of that year, he and his wife helped organize the first major public art exhibition in the City, the widely celebrated Metropolitan Fair. One of many Sanitary Fairs that raised funds for the United States Sanitary Commission (President Lincoln spoke at three of them), the Metropolitan Fair was held in two large buildings near Union Square and was almost entirely produced by the members of the Union League Club. The executive committee consisted of twenty-five wives of Club members who worked with a committee of artists and collectors chaired by the Hudson River School painter and Union League Club member John Frederick Kensett.

So grand that it was described as "like a small World's Fair," the Metropolitan Fair featured displays of American handwork and industry, as well as some European luxuries (a Wall Street tycoon donated $1,000 worth of Parisian finery). More than 350 works of art were loaned or donated, and 196 of them were offered at auction. The impresario Lester Wallack produced theatrical and musical performances, beginning with a spectacular opening night at which a large choir and full orchestra performed. One day, 14,000 tickets to the fair were sold at a then-high price of twenty-five cents. The Metropolitan Fair raised a total of more than $1 million for the Sanitary Commission.

The exhibition's dramatic patriotic centerpiece was a trio of large paintings hung at the end of the main hall, each representing an interpretation of American destiny. One was Frederick Church's grand vista *The Heart of the Andes*, which was interpreted as an appeal to Americans to settle in the South. Facing it across the narrow hall, as though providing an alternate view, was ULC member Albert Bierstadt's *The Rocky Mountains, Lander's Peak*, a highly romanticized impression of the western mountains. This work was widely read as a very different take on national destiny, along the lines of Horace Greeley's famous command, "Go West, young man, go West and grow up with the country." On the

end wall between the two, as though in judgment, was Emanuel Leutze's massive, iconic *Washington Crossing the Delaware*, hanging in a monumental frame embellished with military symbols and heraldry, including a gilded, spread-winged American Eagle over the well-known encomium, "First in war, first in peace, first in the hearts of his countrymen." Supporters of the Union cause understood this great work to mean that, even during a destructive war, the country's institutions of government were empowered to

The Club at the Metropolitan Museum

In 2012, nearly a century and a half after the Union League Club's Metropolitan Fair, these three paintings were rehung in the New American Wing at the Metropolitan Museum of Art. Guided by photographs taken at the fair by Matthew Brady, curators and restoration experts recreated the centerpiece of the Metropolitan Fair exhibit with the paintings in the same relationship with each other, with the immense centerpiece, *Washington Crossing the Delaware*, hung in a replica of its original grand frame.

In a nearby room in the New American Wing, there is another famous American painting with a connection to the Club. This is a dual portrait painted in 1897 by John Singer Sargent of Mr. and Mrs. Isaac N. Phelps Stokes. Shown in the background is Mr. Stokes, an architect and historian of New York. He had grown up in a house on Murray Hill that is now a wing of the Morgan Library & Museum and a neighbor of the Union League Club. The central figure of the painting is his wife, the former Edith Minturn, shown by Sargent to be the personification of the modern woman, exuberant in her energy, beauty, and intelligence. She was granddaughter of the Union League Club's first President.

bring Americans of all sorts and origins together in the common cause of building the country's future. Here was an idea that the Union League Club could support without doubt.[54]

The Metropolitan Fair Gallery attracted thousands of visitors and stimulated a new interest in creating a large, permanent public exhibition hall in the City. "These and many other facts indicate too plainly to be mistaken that the time has come to establish permanent and standard galleries of art, on the most liberal scale, in our large cities," commented an art critic at the time.[55]

One of the Club members who helped organize the Metropolitan Fair was John Jay. On July 4, 1866 he was in Paris at an Independence Day gathering of Americans and their local friends when there arose some discussion of the absence of museums in America. Jay proposed that the Americans who were present draft a proposal for a museum in the form of a memorial to the Union League Club. Jay recalled these events in 1890 in a letter to the Metropolitan Museum's director, Luigi Palma di Cesnola: "The simple suggestion that 'it was time for the American people to lay the foundation of a National Institution and Gallery of Art and that the American gentlemen then in Europe were the men to inaugurate the plan' commended itself to a number of the gentlemen present, who formed themselves into a committee for inaugurating the movement."[56]

Soon, Jay was in a position to move the idea along when he was elected President of the Union League Club, which had organized the Metropolitan Fair. Members of the Club joined with members of the Century Association to form a committee chaired by William Cullen Bryant, the City's cultural leader and a member of both clubs, and including several Union League Club art collectors and artists. The committee and its grand aims gradually developed broad support. Jay remained active until he was appointed U.S. Ambassador to Vienna. Also generating interest in a museum was the Union League Club's Committee on Art, chaired by G.P. Putnam, a book publisher and art collector who donated art to the Club. The proposal to establish the museum was drafted by William J. Hoppin, the Union League's founding Treasurer and later

a Club President (1871 to 1872).

On November 23, 1869, more than 300 people crowded into the theater in the Union League's newly occupied second Clubhouse on Twenty-Sixth Street and, with Bryant in the chair, agreed to found an art museum. Driven by the traditional ideal of personal stewardship for the public good, all agreed that this must be a private effort. When Henry W. Bellows was asked for his opinion, he replied that the price would be high but the need was obvious: "Who can say how soon we may find ourselves the largest and the safest offerers for the custody and protection of the highest of all works in the world?"[57] Money flooded in, Union League Club member Joseph H. Choate assembled the necessary legal papers, and the Metropolitan Museum of Art was officially organized in January 1870. Its first President was Union League Club member John Taylor Johnson, a railroad executive and art collector, and so were the chairman of the executive committee, William T. Blodgett, and four of the artist trustees. When Blodgett went abroad to look for paintings for the museum's collection and discovered that prices were amazingly low, the race to build a first-class museum was on.[58]

The Artists

The Club continued to put on exhibitions organized by artist members, such as John Frederick Kensett and Eastman Johnson (both founders of the Metropolitan Museum), who generously gave time and energy to make the Club a center of art.

The names of the Club's artist members made up a Who's Who of the art world. Kensett established a studio in New York and specialized in rural landscapes, many of them along the shore of the sea or a lake. One of the most respected painters in the Hudson River School, he is represented in major collections of American art. Kensett joined the Union League Club in 1863 and was a leading organizer of the 1864 Metropolitan Fair, and was appointed to the Club's Art and Relics Committee when it was founded a year later ("Relics" was soon dropped from the title.). The brilliant English-born architect and landscape designer Calvert Vaux was working closely with Frederick Law Olmsted on Central Park when he introduced Olmsted to Union League Club founder Henry W. Bellows. After joining the Club, Vaux served on its Art Committee at the time it made early important acquisitions and sponsored significant exhibitions.

Maine-born Eastman Johnson studied painting in Europe for several years before coming to New York. His specialties were rural picturesque paintings, of which *The Wounded Drummer Boy* is an example. A Club member for thirty-seven years, he was a leading figure of the New York art world.

Other artist members included Daniel Huntington, whose portraits of New York's society and political leaders give us a view of his era; Emanuel Leutze, painter of *Washington Crossing the Delaware* and the portrait of Lincoln in the Club's Lincoln Hall; John Quincy Adams Ward, an important sculptor; and George Burroughs Torrey, who painted the dynamic portrait of President Theodore Roosevelt. Among other members, Frederick Remington is well known for his Western themes, Francis Carpenter is identified with his vivid portraits of Lincoln's Cabinet members displayed in the Club's meeting rooms on 3M, and Sanford Robinson Gifford is one of the most respected artists of the Civil War, with 100 paintings of life in the Union Army that include the expansive *Seventh Regiment Encampment Near Washington*, often called *Preaching to the Troops*. Other members were important collectors or dealers, among them Thomas B. Clarke, a specialist in the Hudson River School.

Their contributions to the Club, as well as works by non-members artists, made the Union League Club's reputation as an important home of fine art. Newspaper and magazine updates of the City's art scene included references to "the regular monthly exhibition at the Union League Club." The Club often set aside its traditional Ladies Days, when members' wives and other women relatives visited the Clubhouse, for these shows. In 1908, more than 3,000 viewers visited the Fifth Avenue Clubhouse on two successive Ladies Days to view an exhibition of old masters owned by Club member Henry Clay Frick.[59]

The Crusader with a Drawing Pen

After the Civil War, the Union League Club became extremely active in political reform. This commitment was so firm that in 1866 the Club added a bylaw to its constitution alongside the one for "unqualified loyalty to the United States." The new bylaw said, "It shall be the duty of the Club to resist and expose corruption and promote reform in our National, State, and Municipal affairs and to elevate the ideal of American citizenship." The broad target was political corruption, but the personification of that corruption was William M. Tweed. He had played his cards cleverly during the war, supporting the Union and taking other public stands while building a base of support by helping his mostly immigrant followers avoid the draft. Members of the Union League Club soon saw through these guises and sponsored studies of the Tweed Ring's control of the City. One of these reports stated flat out that "lawlessness, disorganization, pillage, and anarchy" were dominating the City's politics in the 1860s.[60] Another report concluded that the main tasks of City aldermen were "official nominations, accumulations, and division of the spoils of office."[61] The Club pressed for a Congressional investigation of what it called a "naturalization mill" managed by City offices, where more than 27,000 naturalization forms were discovered to be missing.[62]

These massive, meticulously detailed reports had little effect unless public opinion could be mobilized against Tammany Hall. One man made that happen: a Union League Club member, artist, and cartoonist named Thomas Nast. Born in Germany in 1840, the son of a musician in a Bavarian Army Band, Nast emigrated to New York. He dropped out of school at age fifteen when it became clear to his parents and teachers that he had only one interest, which was drawing. Studying the works of John Tenniel and other satirical artists at the English magazine *Punch*, Nast developed a distinctive style that exaggerated the features of his subjects in such a way that their characters could be known without question.

In 1859, Nast moved to the most popular and influential magazine of that time, *Harper's*, which had an intimate connection with

Thomas Nast was literally (and desperately) "out of pocket" when he sent this reply to a Club bill. The cartoon is displayed in the Clubhouse foyer.

Nast's *Lincoln Entering Richmond* shows the crowd paying homage to the President and his son as they walk through the former capitol of the Confederacy.

the Union League Club. Two of the Harper brothers who owned and edited the magazine joined the Club and published pro-Union pamphlets. Nast's first drawing for the magazine exposed a scandal in the police department, which Union League Club members soon reformed. It has been said, "Thomas Nast was a crusader, with a drawing pen instead of a lance."[63] When he covered the Civil War, Nast's woodcuts of camp scenes and Sherman's march to the sea were so effective that Lincoln reportedly referred to him as the Union Army's best recruiting sergeant. Not inclined to take the middle road or be ambivalent, Nast aimed his pen at

The bold idea for the Statue of Liberty originated in France in 1876 with Édouard de Laboulaye's visionary plan. (Edward Harrison May)

The French abolitionist Agenor Étienne de Gasperin publicly supported Abraham Lincoln and prosecution of the Civil War. (Edward Harrison May 1865)

politics. Well-known images of Uncle Sam, the Republican Elephant, the Democratic Donkey, and Santa Claus also originated on his drawing board, but none was as influential as his portrayal of Boss Tweed. Santa and Tweed may have both been chubby, but only one of them was an obvious predator. The destruction of Tweed's reputation is brilliantly summarized in the title of a book about Nast, *Doomed by Cartoon*.

Not one to be subtle, Nast presented Tweed in the guises of a walking money bag and a vulture, and Tammany Hall as a voracious tiger over a caption that read, "The Tammany Tiger Loose:

What Are You Going to Do about It?" The Tammany Tiger cartoon quickly made Nast's reputation and hastened the unmaking of Tweed's. Nast's publishers at *Harper's Weekly* described his drawings at their best as having a "grotesque fidelity." Tweed, upset by Nash's characterization, threatened to horsewhip him. Nast, said his publishers, was "the most cordially hated man in New York—hated by men whose friendship would be a dishonor."[64] Yet he was so respected at the Union League Club that members presented him with a large silver vase celebrating his role and influence during the Civil War. The inscription reads, "Thirty-six members of

Many medallions honoring the new French-American bond
were widely distributed.

This medallion honored the Union League Club's
contributions to the Statue of Liberty.

the Union League Club unite in presenting this vase to Thomas Nast as a token of their admiration of his Genius, and of his ardent devotion of that Genius to the Preservation of his Country from the schemes of Rebellion."[65]

Nast went into semi-retirement at age thirty-nine. After a stake in a western mine melted away, former President Ulysses S. Grant offered him a "sure" investment in his brokerage firm, Grant and Ward, which soon failed. On display in the Club's lobby is a cartoon of Nast's, showing him with empty pockets, drawn and sent in response to a Club appeal for funds.

To reverse his fortune, he branched out. A painting he did of an imagined scene of Lincoln entering Richmond with his son Tad, is displayed in the Club Library. Nast collected the cheery Christmas drawings he had been doing for many years into a book in which the nasty Boss is replaced by a beaming Santa Claus wishing "Merry Christmas to all, and all a good night," and flying off in his sleigh behind the reindeer. Ever the Unionist, Nast also included sketches of bleak Christmases on Civil War battlefields, far from home, where, magically, Santa appears to hand out presents to exhausted soldiers. Hearing of his financial troubles, his

Speaking at the dedication, Chauncey M. Depew (Club President 1886-92) predicted the Statue would welcome strangers "for all time to come." (Wilma Parlaghy)

William M. Evarts (Club President 1882-85) helped propel the dream of "Liberty Enlightening the World" into reality. (Eastman Johnson)

admirer Theodore Roosevelt appointed him Counsel General in Ecuador, where Thomas Nast—artist and American conscience— died in 1902.

Lady Liberty and Grant's Tomb

Later in the nineteenth century, the Club was intimately engaged with the construction of two of America's greatest patriotic monuments. The first was officially called Liberty Enlightening the World, but became known everywhere as the Statue of Liberty. The second is the General Grant National Memorial, popularly known as Grant's Tomb.

The Statue of Liberty was proposed in 1876 by a leading French statesman, Édouard de Laboulaye, to celebrate the long, close relationship between the two republics. France would create and deliver a 151-foot-tall monument to New York, where Americans would install it on a pedestal overlooking the harbor into

Ulysses S. Grant
Members assisted President Grant in his last years, and the Club played a lead role
in building the memorial for him on Riverside Drive.
(Enoch Wood Perry)

General Grant's Tomb

With the Statue of Liberty built and celebrated, the Club became engaged in another large construction project, this one for former President of the United States and General of the Civil War, Ulysses S. Grant. Grant was a frequent visitor to the Club. After his presidency, when his business collapsed, several Union League members contributed to a fund to support him and assist in the publication of his memoirs. After Grant's death, Club President Horace Porter, who had served as Grant's aide de camp during the Civil War, led the drive that raised $600,000 from nearly 90,000 people for the General Grant National Memorial on Riverside Drive in Manhattan.

Horace Porter graduated from West Point in 1860 and went on to serve with great distinction in the Civil War, earning the Medal of Honor for his bravery in the Battle of the Chickamauga. In his memoir "Campaigning with Grant", published in 1897, he recounts his wartime experiences. One of the more interesting is his detailed description of the surrender at Appomattox. During the negotiations, Lee asked to add something to the terms of surrender. Lee had no pencil, so Porter loaned his to Lee. Porter cherished it for the rest of his life.

Porter's account of the surrender includes a description of the scramble for souvenirs as soon as Lee and Grant departed. General Sheridan paid $20 in gold for the small table upon which Grant wrote the terms of surrender, as a gift to the wife of his staff member, General George Armstrong Custer. Years later, on November 21, 1896, Porter gave a speech on the surrender and Mrs. Custer brought it out of storage so the Club could put it on display. The removal of the table from the warehouse was attended by much pomp and ceremony.

At the dedication of Grant's Memorial in 1897, member Grenville M. Dodge served as Grand Marshall of the parade of 60,000 up Riverside Drive. That day the Club hosted a dinner for 1,000 guests and members at its Clubhouse.[70] Later, as Ambassador to France, Porter paid for the transfer of the remains of John Paul Jones to the U.S. Naval Academy.

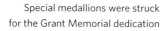

Special medallions were struck for the Grant Memorial dedication

General Horace Porter
(Wilhelm Heinrich Funk)

This medallion is dated December 1863 to commemorate the victories of Vicksburg and Chattanooga.

Metropolitan Fair in 1864.

Each country would raise funds for its part of the grand joint project. The problem was finding the money in America. The project was so novel and ambitious that Americans had trouble imagining the result as anything more than a lighthouse that would benefit only New Yorkers. To stimulate interest and donations, the French sent over the full-scale right hand of Bartholdi's statue, holding a torch, and put it on display in Madison Square Garden. Laboulaye made a point of describing it as "a beacon which enlightens."[66] As Evarts organized fundraising events, Joseph Pulitzer stirred up wide public interest through his newspapers, and enough money was collected to build the pedestal. To honor the Club's cooperation and the centennial of the American Revolution, Bartholdi designed and struck special medallions that he presented to the Club.

On October 28, 1886, an international body of distinguished men and women gathered at the base of the statue for the dedication ceremony, including U.S. President Grover Cleveland and Ferdinand Marie, Vicomte de Lesseps, the developer of the Suez Canal (Laboulaye had died before his ambitious project was completed). The two other speakers were Union League Club members, Evarts and the Club's then President, Chauncey M. Depew. The theme of the day was the friendship of the two republics dating to the American Revolution.

Depew was an old-fashioned orator with many flourishes, and he described the founding of the relationship this way: "The flower of the young aristocracy of France, in their brilliant uniforms, and the farmers and frontiersmen of America, in their faded continentals, bound by a common baptism of blood, became brothers in the knighthood of Liberty."[67]

Those verbal drumbeats heralded the unveiling of the statue before a crowd on the island and the much larger audience looking on from a fleet of ships and boats. By some accounts, Lady Liberty's debut was hastened accidentally. When Evarts took a long pause in the middle of his speech, the men nervously holding the lines to the shroud decided that he had finished and proceeded to give a big pull. As the statue appeared, what was described as "a huge shock

which so many French immigrants sailed.

The people of France donated $250,000 to build the statue of the design of Auguste Bartholdi, a well-known sculptor.

The next requirement was to build a 155-foot pedestal on Bedloe's Island, in New York Harbor. Laboulaye approached the French business community in New York and two clubs with which he was friendly, the Philadelphia Union League and the Union League Club of New York (where Laboulaye's portrait was, and remains, displayed). Members of the Union League Club took leadership positions for the project in America. John Jay, in his second term as Club President, played an important role at first, and the effort came to be guided by two other Union League Club members, former U.S. Secretary of State William Maxwell Evarts and Richard Morris Hunt, one of the country's most successful and influential architects. Hunt's works included many Fifth Avenue mansions and Newport "cottages," and also the façade and Great Hall at the Metropolitan Museum of Art. A founder of the Union League Club, Hunt played a leadership role in the of sound" erupted across the harbor in a spontaneous roar of steam whistles, trumpets, and guns. The statue was briefly visible before it was screened by cannon smoke that lingered for half an hour before Lady Liberty was finally there for all to see and celebrate.[68]

Two reminders of the international effort that created the statue are displayed in the Club. One is the portrait of Edouard de Laboulaye in the Library, the other an elegant vase with an inscription: "Presented to the Union League Club by the Delegation appointed to represent the Republic of France at the inauguration of Bartholdi's Statue, Liberty Enlightening the World."

Another result of the efforts of the members of the Union League Club to create the Statue of Liberty is a stirring sonnet titled "The New Colossus," written in 1893, whose words were inscribed in the pedestal in 1903. It was written for one of the Union League Club's fundraising events for the statue by Emma Lazarus, a thirty-four-year-old writer from an old New York Sephardic Jewish family. Sympathizing with Jewish immigrants fleeing Russian persecution in Russia, she envisioned the new statue as an improved version of the ancient Colossus of Rhodes. She imagined this "Mother of Exiles" proclaiming an invitation:

Give me your tired, your poor,
Your huddled masses yearning to breathe free,
The wretched refuse of your teeming shore.
Send these, the homeless, tempest-tost to me,
I lift my lamp beside the golden door!

Chauncey Depew understood her point exactly: "The Statue would for all time to come welcome the incoming stranger."[69]

This elegant vase was one of many French gifts
to the Club when the Statue of Liberty was dedicated.

The Union League Club, 1863–2013

Cheerful Hospitality Afforded

The first of the Union League Club's four Clubhouses was a modest private home leased from a man named Parish and located on East Seventeenth Street, just off Broadway on the north side of Union Square, not far from many members' homes at Madison Square and Gramercy Park. The Clubhouse's opening day, May 12, 1863, was also the first Ladies Day, an event the Club historically reserved for grand occasions. The Club handed out 350 tickets, each good for a member and three guests, only two of whom, Strong was pleased to report, were Copperheads.

Opposite: *Reception at the Old Union League Club, Madison Square* (E. L. Henry, 1888?)

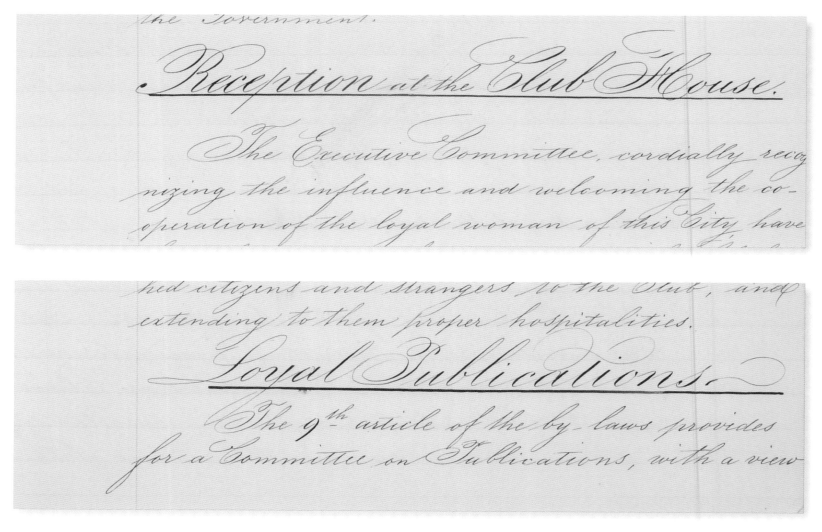

the Government.

Reception at the Club House.

The Executive Committee, cordially recognizing the influence and welcoming the co-operation of the loyal woman of this City have

hed citizens and strangers to the Club, and extending to them proper hospitalities.

Loyal Publications.

The 9th article of the by-laws provides for a Committee on Publications, with a view

Minutes describing the first annual Open House for the Ladies

This interim Clubhouse needed improvement. There was no dining room or kitchen, but the members made do with catered meals that they ate in the meeting area, where they gathered to hear the news from the battlefields. Smaller rooms were set aside for meetings of the Executive Committee, the Committee on Political Reform, and the Art Committee, and for a small library that quickly became crowded with thousands of political pamphlets plus piles of scrap books of the Civil War compiled by an energetic member, Thomas Seaman Townsend. Like any good club, the Parish house had a bar (called the "wine room") and areas set aside for the members' tables for their pursuits of billiards, whist, and especially dominoes, the favorite gentleman's indoor game of the nineteenth century. "From the earliest years of the Union League Club at least one table of dominoes was actively occupied each morning, noon, and night in the old Union Square Clubhouse," wrote an earlier Club historian, Will Irwin. "By established custom, one quartet of elderly contenders would preempt the table for a morning session, another quartet would take possession for a midday set-to, still another quartet would put on a domino matinee, and a fourth quartet would often play into the wee small hours."[71] Dominoes was eventually succeeded as the Club's game of choice by billiards, contract bridge, and squash.

The Parish house remained insufficient for the needs of the membership, which very rapidly neared 1,000 men, many of whom stopped by regularly to play dominoes, gossip, philosophize, and trade rumors about the progress of the war. Seeing a need for a larger building, member and architect Richard Morris Hunt produced plans for a mammoth, intimidating building that he wanted to build at Madison Square on an ambitious scheme to let out the ground floor for shops and place the Club's facilities in the upper stories. This plan was put on hold, and later dropped, due to concerns about taking on more debt on top of the $30,000 that had already been borrowed to pay for furniture and improvements. Excess debt had done in other clubs, especially as the membership suffered a post-war decline due to what Henry W. Bellows called (no doubt with great disappointment) "the decrease of excitement in political matters."[72] Everybody's spirits were soon revived by the appearance of a new cause, which was the fight against Boss Tweed, and the membership blossomed to 1,263 in 1868, including more than 200 non-resident members—a sign that the Club had a national following.

Another reason for the delay in moving to a larger and more elaborate building was the deep affection that members felt for the Parish house. Though its amenities may have been limited, the experiences associated with it were profound. This was the place that members defended during the Draft Riots, and that hosted the spectacular review of the Twentieth U.S. Colored Regiment. Here, in November 1864, the building was crowded with men and women poring over telegraph reports from the election. In April 1865, the members packed the Parish house twice—first

joyfully to hear the news from Appomattox Courthouse and then, a few days later (as men wept uncontrollably) to try to absorb the reports from Washington, where Lincoln lay dying. These events defined the Club both then and throughout its long history. When the move eventually came, the Executive Committee agreed on this statement honoring "the memories and traditions of this house":

"Here we commenced, and, during all the dark days we have passed through, have lived and labored. There is no corner of this house which has not a record of faithful work done, and cheerful hospitality afforded. Here we have labored for the good cause, and here the other workers, members of the nation, have been our guests. What kindly remembrances for us, and them, and how long the list of those who, when we leave these walls, must go out with us. Old age, chance, and accident will have turned away the feet of many, whom we most delight to honor.[73]"

The Mansion

Requiring ever more space for its rapidly growing membership and lengthening agenda of activities, in April 1868, the Club moved nine blocks uptown into larger rented premises on Twenty-Sixth Street, near Madison Avenue. This building was a mansion in the French Second Empire style that member Leonard Jerome had built for his own use. He became the grandfather of Winston Churchill after his daughter, Jennie, married the second son of the Duke of Marlborough. Jerome was one of New York's most vivid and storied characters. A sportsman of Gilded Age ambitions, he built a racetrack in the Bronx called Jerome Park, owned and raced yachts and horses, wagered large sums on both and on cards, and also took big gambles on securities, not all of which he won. One of the many tales about him has Jerome giving a dinner to a crowd of friends when a telegram arrived. Jerome read it, looked up, and announced, "Gentlemen, I'm a poor man, but don't worry about the check. I paid for dinner in advance." The ever wary George Templeton Strong referred to Jerome as "not the saint but the stockjobber," and to his mansion as "Theatre San Jeronimo."[74]

When the Club opened the new Clubhouse on Fifth Avenue in 1881, the *Times* praised it as "far and away the city's grandest."

entrances, allowed the Club to lease it out. A reception for General Ulysses S. Grant in 1867 was so large that a temporary floor had to be laid outside under a canopy.[75]

Jerome never could quite afford the place, which was why he often rented it out to one club or another. The cost of leasing and furnishing the building was covered by an issue of $50,000 in bonds (the equivalent today of $875,000), most of which was picked up by a few members. The Club retired most of the bonds within two years.

A contemporary clubman praised the Jerome mansion as "probably, internally as well as externally, the most elegant clubhouse in the city, as it is the most expensively upholstered. The general framework of the furnishing is of black walnut, though the larger mirror frames are of rosewood."[76]

The food was splendidly presented. A menu from a banquet in 1872 was described by Club historian Will Irwin as reading "like the libretto of an epicurean grand opera," running from *Purée des Pois Vertes* and a *Château d'Yquem* through many courses to *Glâce Napolitaine* and a *Clos de Vougex*. On the back of the menu, scribbled in pencil, was a poem that opened, "We may live without poetry, music, art" and ended, "But civilized men cannot live without cooks."[77] With such Gilded Age stylishness, there was no wonder that the new Clubhouse was often packed. After returning home from the opening party at the Jerome mansion, on April 16, 1868, George Templeton Strong summed up the evening: "Many nice people, great crowd, and heat unbearable."[78]

Art Helpful to the Cause

The Jerome mansion's walls filled up with the rapidly enlarging art collection. The new artistic interest was acceptable to the founders, but with qualifications. The hard-line political figure Henry Bellows, in his history of the early years, urged the Union League Club not to stray from its original mission as laid down in the certificate of incorporation in 1865: "to promote, encourage, and sustain, by all proper means, absolute and unqualified loyalty to the Government of the United States." Bellows viewed

Jerome had been planning the sprawling structure for many years, first buying the land at the southeast corner of Madison Avenue and Twenty-Sixth Street, in what at that time was a wilderness far north of Union Square, and using it for several years as a winter skating rink as he assembled the cash and loans to pay for this great house, with its fifty feet of frontage on Madison Avenue, 175 feet on the street, and a total area of 8,750 square feet. There were spacious billiard and card rooms, a bowling alley, plenty of space for dining and meeting, fountains, and a spacious room in the back called the Theater, which seated 600 for lectures, accommodated a 1,000 for grand occasions, and, because it had its own

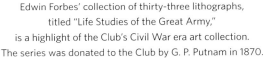

Edwin Forbes' collection of thirty-three lithographs,
titled "Life Studies of the Great Army,"
is a highlight of the Club's Civil War era art collection.
The series was donated to the Club by G. P. Putnam in 1870.

art as a handmaiden to the founders' political agenda. The Club, he wrote, "should unquestionably, both in its library and art collection, persistently cultivate the specialty of Loyalty and Union, by carefully collecting what best illustrates them, leaving to other associations what is more general, and, though interesting in itself, not directly helpful to the cause to which the past history of this club has pledged its members."

The Art Committee agreed: there should be "a special character to the art collection of this Club, namely, a patriotic and historical motive, in which the purpose should be to preserve and perpetuate, by the aid of art, the memory of the great struggle that had saved and recreated the Union and the Nation."[79] In this spirit, the Union League Club collected art on political and patriotic themes. The subjects of the many portraits acquired in the Club's first twenty years included Lincoln, Union Army Generals William T.

Sherman and Philip Sheridan, and English and European political reformers such as John Bright, Richard Cobden, and Édouard de Laboulaye (who played an important role in the Club history with his proposal for the Statue of Liberty), and the Club's Presidents.

The Club also made a point of acquiring illustrations of Civil War military life. One treasure is the set of etchings by Edwin Forbes, showing the details of a soldier's life, that originally ran in *Frank Leslie's Magazine* and are now displayed on floor 3M, in the halls outside the Cabinet Rooms. Other battlefield art by Jasper Cropsey, Eastman Johnson, Sanford Robinson Gifford, and Winslow Homer also came into the collection. Homer's *Skirmish in the Wilderness* represented the furious fighting in the underbrush and among the trees in the battle that brought Ulysses S. Grant to prominence. This work remained in the collection until 1938, when it was sold, reportedly because it did not fit (either physically

This portrait of Richard Cobden is in the Club's special collection
relating to English and European political thinkers.
(Giuseppe Fagnini)

Union League Club Clubhouse, 5th Avenue at 39th Street
(Katherine Merrill)

NEW YORK CITY—THE PRESIDENTIAL VISIT—RECEPTION GIVEN TO PRESIDENT AND MRS. HAYES IN THE THEATRE OF THE UNION LEAGUE CLUB, FRIDAY EVENING, DECEMBER 21ST.—SEE PAGE 307.

Reception honoring President and Mrs. Rutherford B. Hayes at the Madison Avenue Clubhouse.
Illustration courtesy of Edward and Austin Hayes from *Frank Leslie's Illustrated Newspaper*, January 8, 1878.

or stylistically) in the new Park Avenue Clubhouse. It is now in the Connecticut Museum of American Art in New Britian. [80]

In 1870, the Union League Club was only seven years old, yet owned 126 works of art with a total value of $19,000 (the equivalent of $325,000 today), including thirty-seven oils (seventeen of them portraits and most of the rest military subjects). Even with these expenditures, the Club was solvent. In fact, that year it made a $600 profit. The leading sources of its income then and throughout most of its history were in four categories: dues and initiation fees ($60 and $100 in 1870); the restaurant; the bar; and the cigar stand in the lobby. In 1870 alone, sales of cigars, cigarettes, and pipe tobacco brought in $8,664.29, the equivalent of nearly $150,000 today. [81]

Although the Club was doing well, the times were unsteady and the officers were cautious about moving out of rented quarters and building a clubhouse. Following a Wall Street crash in 1873, many New York clubs that had taken out mortgages and built buildings failed rapidly. The Union League Club bided its time in the Jerome mansion and waited for better times, eventually moving out in 1881. The Jerome mansion later was home briefly to the University Club, the New York Yacht Club, and the Jockey Club, and then for many years to the Manhattan Club. The framework of the Theater's façade was still visible in the 1940s, and it was over a century old when it was granted landmark status in 1965. Efforts to restore it to its old glamour ended when nobody could come up with the $850,000 purchase price, and this historic home of clubs was taken down in 1967, ninety-nine years after the Union League Club made it the Club's second home.

A Young Man's Club

With many members coming in and pressing to expand the mission beyond politics into social activities, the Club's popularity grew and the membership cap was raised to 1,500 to shorten the waiting list. The Jerome mansion, meanwhile, was regularly crowded and in need of alterations. After camping out in rental spaces for fifteen years, in 1879, the members agreed to build a custom-designed clubhouse to fit their needs.

The Club issued $125,000 in bonds, raised the initiation fee to $300, and leased a plot of land on the northeast corner of Thirty-Ninth Street and Fifth Avenue, where a riding stable stood. This seemed a big leap, far uptown, but this was the City's great era of club formation. "The Clubs are more frequented than ever, and there are more of them," observed a commentator, adding, "Every division into which men may be separated now has its club."[82] There were clubs for artists and actors, for yachtsmen and businessmen and women, for college graduates and many national origins. The Union League Club stood almost alone for being defined largely by political convictions.

The popularity of clubs and the prominence of the Union League Club combined to stimulate lengthy speculation about what, exactly, was the appropriate appearance for a New York men's club. On one hand, there were commentators who wanted to see a dignified, thoroughly classical building. On the other hand, an architect declared that, while the design of the clubhouse's interior should be suitable for the Club's "quiet retiring side," the exterior should energetically blend "somewhat of pretentious show" with the look of a comfortable private home.[83] The second proposal is a fair description of the clubhouse that was built.

The winner of the competition among nine architects, Robert Peabody, of the Boston firm of Peabody & Stearns, was described as "a confirmed eclectic at heart" and was known for designing large, elegant buildings in a variety of styles, from Newport "cottages" to Manhattan office buildings.[84] After a visit to the Jerome mansion and an introduction to the Club by Henry W. Bellows, Peabody went back to Boston and began sketching. The result was a lively, handsome building in a loose Queen Anne style, with multiple gables, many horizontal bands of different colors, overhanging eaves, monumental chimneys, a fence on the roof reminiscent of a colonial New England captain's walk, and large, attractive, cleverly designed windows in the upper stories that both afforded a sweeping view of the street and protected the privacy of the members inside. Other features in the original plans included a gazebo on the roof and a bowling alley in the basement under the Fifth Avenue sidewalk. The Union League accepted the design with pleasure (although it did reject the gazebo and, for the time being, the bowling alley).

It was a large building, with an area of 13,538 square feet, half again as large as the Jerome mansion, and eighty-four feet of frontage on Fifth Avenue. The dining room was twice the length of the old one, and the social area, called the Members Hall, could have held the old Theater with space to spare. Scattered through that large space were a few intimate gathering areas. An alcove off the Main Dining Room was a favorite site of small meetings, and so were some seats in the Library under windows designed by John La Farge and Louis Comfort Tiffany that were also seen in other parts of the Club. La Farge also contributed a dramatic gold leaf, bas-relief Winged Victory to the new clubhouse. By 1886, Librarian Ellsworth Totten was presiding over a collection so large that the catalog, published and widely distributed by Club member G.P. Putnam, ran 451 pages.

The new clubhouse's striking appearance and practical interior arrangement helped establish the Union League Club's image as an energetic, contemporary institution. While some traditionalists condemned Peabody's design as too busy ("The edifice seems an architectural negation of repose," one of them asserted), others praised it for its vitality. "It is not a conservative club," said an enthusiastic reviewer. "It is a progressive, alert club, a young man's club."[85]

It also was an elegant club. The *Times*, whose editor and business manager were Union League Club members, called the new clubhouse "far and away the city's grandest as well as comparable in scale and facilities to the most lavish of London's celebrated clubs."[86] The opinion that may have meant the most came from someone who simply liked the building's friendly appearance. After happening by the Club on a hot summer's day, when awnings were put out over the wide windows, the reporter expressed his personal appreciation for the "domestic look of the big and costly building before us."[87] The clubhouse *looked* comfortable, and for the people inside, it *was* comfortable, too.

Here the Union League Club happily lived for fifty years, from 1881 until the present-day clubhouse was constructed on Murray Hill in 1931.

The Library was one of the most admired rooms in the Fifth Avenue Clubhouse.
Its influence can be seen in the Park Avenue building's Library. (Otto Stark)

The Union League Club, 1863–2013

The Style of the Club

Although the Club's officers and architect believed they understood the needs and wishes of the members, two lapses in the design were quickly identified and corrected. Assuming that Club members wished to socialize in either very large or very small gatherings, Peabody laid out the new Fifth Avenue building like a traditional clubhouse, with some expansive spaces and some intimate ones but little in between. After some members complained that there were no spaces where they could take small groups of guests, the Club within a year and at considerable expense converted a set of bedrooms on the third floor for use for members' private functions.

Opening off the same hallway, with an adjoining kitchen and some rooms interconnected by doors, this suite seems to have been similar in use to the Cabinet rooms on 3M in the Club today. These five rooms were named the Gold, Blue, Olive, Tapestry, and Moorish, each with unique highlighting but using the same color scheme, which was described as blue, black, and corn. Clearly members were expecting more of their club.[88]

Opposite: *Club Corner*
(Childe Hassam, 1893)

The second lapse was the decision not to build a bowling alley. The Club's younger members told their seniors that they wanted physical activity. There was billiards, of course—"The Billiards Room became the heart of the Club," claimed one historian of the Union League—but that is a game, not an athletic sport.[89] The alley was added and bowling became popular, with extensive league play with other clubs. This was not the only exercise available in the building. One member refused to take the elevator, preferring to hike up and down the grand staircase. On the other end of the exercise spectrum were the men sometimes called "the window loungers," who sat and occasionally snoozed in the overstuffed chairs placed near the wide windows projecting out over Fifth Avenue. These gentlemen were gently parodied in cartoons in *The New Yorker* and other magazines.

The Club was well known for having and displaying a distinctive style. Almost from the beginning, the Union League Club monogram was displayed throughout the Club, including on china and glassware. The staff was well turned out, as a writer reported in 1873: "Employees of the Club are expected to appear in full dress on all occasions—with the exception of ushers, who are in uniform, and the superintendent, who is at liberty to dress in the manner of a private gentleman."[91]

By the 1880s, most employees of the Club were black men. They were a cohesive group that held annual gatherings at a restaurant theater called Lyric Hall, on Forty-Second Street near Sixth Avenue. Among them were sons of slaves, former Pullman porters, and veterans of the Civil War Colored Regiments. One of the longest-serving staff members, William Seldon Miles, was born a slave in Virginia. Named for his owner, he was taken north after Abraham Lincoln signed the Emancipation Proclamation (which Miles referred to as "the paper"), and at age twenty, he started work as a bell boy at the Fifth Avenue Clubhouse in its first year, 1881.[92]

Another African American staff member, George H. Griffin, was formerly the butler for Samuel L. Clemens, who described Griffin as "shrewd, wise, polite, always good-natured, cheerful to

The Monthly Meeting

For many members, nothing exemplified the glory of the small republic of the Union League Club more or better than the members' meeting. Held monthly except in summer into the 1930s, the members' dinner played a central role in the style and life of the Club. There, friendships were made or revived, new members were elected by old ones, new policies were approved or voted down, and speakers addressed major issues. Occasionally, the members would engage in a debate (usually polite but sometimes bitter) on a Club or national matter. Tradition and ceremony ruled the evening. A newspaper reported on the last meeting held at the Fifth Avenue clubhouse before the Club moved to the Park Avenue clubhouse in 1931:

"For fifty years an old-fashioned dinner bell has summoned the members to meetings and dinners, and last night it rang in the old halls for the last time. An attendant had no sooner passed through the rooms and hall on the ground floor ringing the bell when the members, some over eighty years of age, began to climb the red-carpeted stairway to the assembly hall, where the dinner was held.

Members who had joined in the first celebrations in the Clubhouse and walked up these stairs in the buoyancy and freshness of youth, after a long lapse of time now ascended them slowly with the aid of canes and paused on the top step for breath. . . . The banquet hall was bright with the red of carnations, which made a centerpiece for each table, while paintings of famous members . . . looked down from the walls soon to be razed. The speakers' table was under the huge portrait of Lincoln, by Leutze, said to be the finest painting of the Emancipator in America, around which were massed the national colors.[90]

As usual, the meeting ended with a group singing of 'America.'"

gaiety, honest, religious, a cautious truth-speaker, devoted friend to the family." Griffin may have been an inspiration for the runaway slave Jim in *The Adventures of Huckleberry Finn*. When Clemens lost his money in bad investments in 1891, he approached the Union League Club about giving Griffin a job. Griffin served as a waiter in the dining room for nearly six years while working on the side as a private banker, loaning funds to waiters (and, reportedly, members who were behind on their Club bills). In May 1897, George Griffin suffered a heart attack and died at the Club late one night after serving dinner. The Club contributed to the funeral expenses.[93]

The Union League probably employed more black men than most other predominately white clubs in the city. This was due in large part to the long history of personal commitment by the Club's members to African Americans during the Civil War and the Draft Riots, as well as to the Union League Club's political stance. In 1902, the officers proposed that the staff be integrated and the black staff cut back. However, when the question was taken to a vote at a Club meeting, the proposal was defeated by a margin of three to one.

Around the turn of the century, there was so much public interest in clubs that New York newspapers ran regular columns with titles like "Heard in the Smoking Room" that passed on news and gossip. Inevitably, there was speculation about the attributes that made some people attractive to membership committees. A new word, "clubbable," was coined to describe men who made the grade. A clubbable man was congenial, tactful, friendly but not raucous, dependable but not subservient, and, above all, willing and able to fit in with the larger group, whatever that group's special interests. "A club means comfort, ease, and good fellowship under restrictions which do not seem hard to bear to those who, by seeking membership, accept them," observed a writer at the time.[94]

Clubbability had its limits. Whether Frederick Law Olmsted, Henry W. Bellows, Wolcott Gibbs, or the other opinionated founders of the Union League Club were clubbable good

The mailbox was brought over to Park Avenue from the Fifth Avenue Clubhouse.

fellows is an open question. Making a religion of patriotism, as Bellows urged, can be a lonely task. Controversy was a fact of their lives, and so was politics. Club Presidents were expected to address national or local political issues in their speeches at members' meetings, there were regular reports from members who were active in public affairs, and from time to time the assembled members voted on a resolution regarding national policy.

Members who tried to shift interest away from politics were reminded that, under its constitution, the Club's "primary object" was to rebuke disloyalty to the United States and the secondary

Fireplace designed for the Fifth Avenue Clubhouse now graces the Mary Murray Lounge.
Fountain brought from the Fifth Avenue Clubhouse.

one was "to resist and expose corruption and promote reform in our National, State, and Municipal affairs and to elevate the ideal of American citizenship." To attend to these aims and the business of the Club, the Union League developed an elaborate system of governance, with a President, twelve Vice Presidents, and an executive committee, all elected by the members, subject to term limits, and held accountable by the members at regular meetings, which were held monthly until 1937.

Of the standing committees, the most powerful was the Committee on Political Reform. It was designated to carry on the concerns and spirit of the founders, while reminding members of the principles and experiences that served as the Union League Club's anchor and chain. One of the last large events at the Jerome mansion, in May 1880, was a gathering of 143 surviving members who joined the Club in its first eighteen months, during the Civil War. At the head table were two men indelibly identified with the cause: former Club President John Jay and Honorary Member

William Tecumseh Sherman. Sixteen toasts were offered. If any of the speakers observed the guideline to keep their comments to ten minutes, it is not clear in the transcript. All looked back to the trying days of the war. Henry Bellows spoke on "The Work and Charities of the Club," George Bliss, the commander of the Twentieth Regiment, addressed the topic, "The Colored Regiments," and former President Jackson Schultz' topic was "The Loyal Merchants of New York," of whom he was one at a time when the majority of New York merchants opposed President Lincoln and the War. The U.S. Army was toasted by General Sherman, and "The Loyal Women of America" by former Club President Joseph H. Choate.[95]

With these great concerns so prominent not only in the Club's past but also in its present, some might have thought that smaller issues would be ignored. Yet no topic was too slight to be ignored by the Committee on Political Reform. One enthusiastic member of the committee, Elizur Brace Hinsdale, wrote so many reports and letters to editors about the minutiae of political reform that they filled a 325-page book.[96] Tiring of the great volume of minor controversies, in 1889, the committee's chairman, Whitelaw Reid, publisher of the *New York Tribune*, proposed a new policy for the committee. "Only subjects of immediate and vital interest should be submitted," he wrote, "to the end that the influence of the Club may not be dissipated by too frequent utterances on minor matters, or on points where investigation and discussion of the members have not brought a decided majority of the members to one mind."[97] Reid's committee report that year ran less than two pages, one-third the length of his predecessor's, yet Hinsdale and his fellow committee members soon resumed their investigations.

With politics playing such a dominant role in the Club's agenda, the admissions policy was bound to be affected by it. What a Club historian tactfully called "the caution and suspicion necessary during the war years" survived for many years, and Democrats and former Copperheads had trouble being admitted to the Club.[98] While membership in the Republican Party was not required as a condition of membership, there was a general rule that was expressed in a resolution agreed on at a members meeting in the 1870s: "The Club expresses the hope that the Committee on Admissions will not report for admission the name of any person whose views on public questions do not in their opinion agree with the principles of the Republican Party hitherto expressed."[99] That was the guide through most of the Club's history.

Political conviction was not the only membership issue. In the 1880s, social status, including opinions about people's ethnicity, became a frequently voiced concern in New York. Mrs. Astor's exclusive Club of the 400 was well known and widely influential. In many clubs, groups of younger members favored more restrictive standards based on their notions of "clubbability." Blackballing was facilitated by the Union League Club's original rule that it took negative votes by only ten percent of members at a Club meeting to reject a candidate for membership. As more candidates were rejected, the Club turned for advice to a respected younger member, Elihu Root. Root persuaded the Club to raise the bar to

one-third of the members present, and also to enlarge the Committee on Admissions so that a single member's personal prejudice had less effect.

These changes in the bylaws did not prevent a wave of blackballing after 1890. One group tried and failed to blackball the well-known tycoon and art collector Henry Clay Frick after he moved to New York from Pittsburgh. There also were contested elections for the Admissions Committee and Executive Committee, and, in 1900, the Club's first disputed election for President led to the defeat of the candidate of the Nominating Committee by a challenger.

All these events were reported in the City's newspapers. In 1893, the son of a longtime member, Jesse Seligman, was rejected for membership. One of three brothers who were German-Jewish commercial bankers and Union League Club members for many years, Jesse Seligman had supported the Republican Party, served on prestigious Club committees, and was elected for a term as a Union League Club Vice President. He was present at the meeting where his son's candidacy was rejected. When the result of the vote was announced, Seligman, in tears, rose to his feet and resigned from the Club.

The Spanish-American War

Although many New York businessmen opposed war with Spain, the sinking of the *Maine* in February 1898 sparked a firestorm of aggression fueled by sensationalist newspapers. The members' support of the declaration of war by President William McKinley was brought about by the efforts of Club member and Assistant Secretary of the Navy Theodore Roosevelt.

During the brief conflict, the Clubhouse was often filled with uniformed men from the American and other armies and navies. At luncheon lectures by officers and journalists, the members learned about the achievements of Roosevelt and the Rough Riders, the successes of the African-American regiment known as the Buffalo Soldiers, and the victories of the Navy in Cuban and Philippine waters.

President William McKinley
(W. D. Murphy, 1903)

One day, a U.S. Navy Captain repeated Admiral George Dewey's sharp response to the German commanding officer who had initiated a formal complaint about the American occupation of Manila Bay. Dewey snapped, "Tell Admiral Diederichs that I control this bay and my orders must be obeyed! And tell Admiral Diederichs that if he wants a fight he can have it right now."[100] A reporter who was present wrote up the anecdote without the speaker's or the Club's permission, and to Dewey's embarrassment, it was spread across the country. After that, the Club was more circumspect about allowing newspapermen in the building without invitations.

When news of Dewey's victory in the Philippines reached New York, the Club exuberantly decorated the front with bunting and placed stacks of shields with American flags prominently above the windows on Fifth Avenue, topping each display with the image of an American eagle. Former Club President Richard P. Phelan described the display in one of his "History Corner" columns in the Club *Bulletin*: "From roof to ground dropped seven streamers of red, white, and blue bunting, over which were distributed 600 incandescent lamps. The centerpiece was an illumination in white of the single name, 'Dewey,' surrounded by an eagle with outstretched wings."[101]

The Union League Club may have been changing in some ways, but its members always loved a patriotic celebration.

Honorary Members 1864–1893

Honorary Member	Elected to Honorary Membership	Admitted to Regular Membership (if applicable)	Notable Achievements
Abraham Lincoln	April 14, 1864		President of the United States
Ulysses S. Grant	April 14, 1864		President of the United States
Robert Anderson	April 14, 1864		Major General
George G. Meade	April 14, 1864		Major General
Ambrose E. Burnside	June 9, 1864		Major General
Winfield S. Hancock	June 9, 1864		Major General, United States Army
William T. Sherman	June 9, 1864		General, United States Army
Philip H. Sheridan	June 9, 1864		Lieutenant General, United States Army
Horatio G. Wright	June 9, 1864		Major General, United States Army
Gouverneur K. Warren	June 9, 1864		Major General, United States of America
William F. Smith	June 9, 1864		Major General
George H. Thomas	June 9, 1864		Major General, United States Army
David G. Farragut	December 9, 1865		Admiral, United States Navy
David D. Porter	December 14, 1865		Vice Admiral, United States Navy
Theodorus Bailey	December 14, 1865		Rear Admiral, United States Navy
John Rodgers	December 14, 1865		Commodore, United States Navy
Andrew Johnson	1866		President of the United States
George Templeton Strong	March 28, 1867	February 21, 1863	Lawyer and diarist; Founder, Union League Club
Oliver O. Howard	March 9, 1871		Major General, United States Army
Melancthon Smith	November 9, 1871		Rear Admiral, United States Navy
Henry L. Kendrick	1891	1882	Colonel, United States Army
Henry W. Bellows	March 11, 1880	February 21, 1863	Reverend for the Unitarian Church and President of the United States Sanitary Commission Founder, Union League Club
Peter Cooper	January 13, 1881	March 6, 1863	Industrialist, philanthropist and founder of Cooper Union
Chester A. Arthur	October 13, 1881	1868	President of the United States
Morrison R. Waite	March 9, 1882		United States Supreme Court Chief Justice
Cornelius R. Agnew	October 12, 1882	February 21, 1863	Surgeon General of New York State, Founder of Columbia School of Mines, Brooklyn Eye & Ear Hospital, and Manhattan Eye & Ear Hospital Founder, Union League Club
Oliver Wolcott Gibbs	October 12, 1882	February 21, 1863	Chemist and President of the National Academy of Sciences Founder, Union League Club
Frederick Law Olmstead	October 12, 1882	February 21, 1863	Landscape architect and Executive Secretary of the United States Sanitary Commission Founder, Union League Club
George B. Butler	March 13, 1884	1867	Chemist and President of the National Academy of Sciences Chairman, Political Reform Committee, Union League Club
Hamilton Fish	January 8, 1885	1878	Union League Club President 1879 Secretary of State of the United States
John Ericsson	May 14, 1885		Designer of the USS Monitor
John M. Schofield	November 11, 1886		Lieutenant General, United States Army
Benjamin Harrison	January 10, 1889		President of the United States
William J. Hoppin	February 14, 1889	February 21, 1863	Secretary of the American Legation in London and Union League Club President 1871–1872 Founder, Union League Club
John Jay	May 14, 1891	1863	Union League Club President 1866–1869 and 1877, Envoy Extraordinary and Minister Plenipotentiary to Austria-Hungary
Le Grand B. Cannon	January 14, 1892	February 21, 1863	Colonel, United States Army, Founder of the Union League Club
William M. Evarts	February 9, 1893	1863	Union League Club President 1882–1885 Secretary of State of the United States, United States Senator
Chauncey M. Depew	February 9, 1893	1868	Union League Club President 1886–1892, United States Senator
Levi P. Morton	February 9, 1893	1863	Vice President of the United States

The Union League

THE REGIMENTAL COAT OF ARMS

SEE IT THROUGH

The EAGLE symbolizes the United States of America.

The CROSSED RIFLES mean Infantry.

The BUFFALO HEAD signifies colored soldier, because in frontier days the Indians used to call our colored soldiers "Buffalo Soldiers," because in color they were black or brown like the Buffalo, and like the Buffalo they were good fighters, as the Indians had learned from experience.

The REGIMENTAL MOTTO, "See It Through," expresses the spirit, the soul of the Regiment.

The LAUREL LEAVES typify victory,—the victory that the Regiment will always bend every effort to achieve, and for which it will willingly make every sacrifice.

THEODORE ROOSEVELT
From his youth onwards, "T.R." is closely advised by senior Club members who are also national figures, Joseph H. Choate and Elihu Root.

1901

WORLD WAR I
All three candidates for the Republican Presidential nomination in 1916 are Club members who urge that the country to declare war on Germany. When it finally does, the Club throws itself into the war effort.

1916

THE BUFFALO SOLDIERS AND THE HARLEM HELLFIGHTERS
One of the many members in uniform, Col. William Hayward trains and leads the highly decorated Harlem Hellfighters "colored" regiment.

1917

ENTERING THE FRAY
Causes taken on by the Club and its members include the American Red Cross and the successful fight against Prohibition led by former Club President Elihu Root.

1920

in the 20ᵀᴴ Century

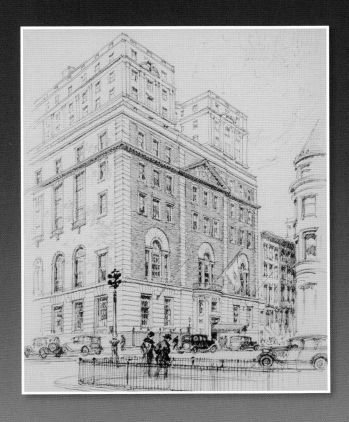

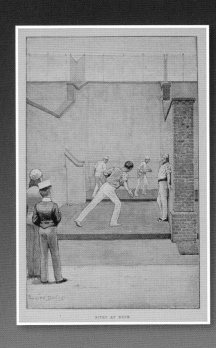

**FAREWELL
TO FIFTH AVENUE**
As the old Clubhouse is vacated, the Club President recalls "the comfortable, happy, and, on occasion, uproarious times we have had," adding, "Presidents of the United States have spoken from the rostrum."

1931

A GRAND STATEMENT
The handsome new Park Avenue Clubhouse on Murray Hill has many of the old building's features, with the addition of squash courts and a very successful Ladies Dining Room and Lounge.

1931

GAMES AND HOBBIES
Long considered "the heart of the Club," billiards now competes with dominoes, cards, squash, bowling and other games. The members are looked after by the loyal staff.

1935

T.R. and the Union League Club

There were always a few members of vivid personality and powerful ambition who were especially noteworthy both in and outside the doors of the Clubhouse. One of the best known in the Club's 150-year history is Theodore Roosevelt, whose name is on one of the Union League's most important awards. For all that has been written about the remarkable "T.R.," little has mentioned his intense relationship with the Union League Club and the three other prominent members who inspired and advised him. They were his father, Theodore Roosevelt, Sr., and Club Presidents Joseph H. Choate and Elihu Root.

Roosevelt knew the Club from boyhood. "I went to the Union Leaug Club," eleven-year-old Theodore Roosevelt wrote in his childhood diary in 1870, misspelling for probably the last time the name of the organization that launched and often supported his political career.[102] He would have been taken to the Jerome mansion Clubhouse by "the best man I ever knew," his beloved father who "combined strength and courage with gentleness, tenderness, and great unselfishness."[103] Motivated by a powerful sense of stewardship, the father built hospitals, co-founded the American Museum of Natural History with J. Pierpont Morgan, created the allotment system that kept food on the tables of soldier's families, and was active in numerous charities.

Opposite: *Theodore Roosevelt*
(George Burroughs Torrey, 1905)

The son built the U.S. Navy and the Panama Canal, renewed the Republican Party (and then split it), and, in his flexible anti-trust and labor policies, improved relations between big and small businesses and their workers. They shared a vitality that was noted by anybody who spent time with them. A family friend, Louisa Schuyler, remembered the senior Roosevelt, in full evening dress, gracefully serving dinner to a group of poor boys in a shelter "and later dashing off to an evening party in Fifth Avenue." As for the son, the novelist Edith Wharton described him as "so alive at all points, and so gifted with the rare faculty of living intensely and entirely in every moment as it passed."[104] Inevitably there were differences: the father was an idealist, the son a pragmatist. Otherwise, they were the same man, right down to their membership in the Union League Club, where the father all but resided and which served as the son's frame of reference.

When Theodore Sr. died, evidently of stomach cancer, at age forty-six in 1877, into the breach in T.R.'s life stepped Joseph H. Choate, a close friend of the senior Roosevelt's whose term as Club President had expired. A prominent lawyer and leading political figure and diplomat, Choate had saved the lives of more than one African American during the Draft Riots. Choate had a sharp tongue. "Who is that impudent young man?" Henry W. Bellows demanded upon first seeing the young Choate in action.[105]

Choate became one of the country's most popular public speakers (another was Chauncey Depew, the Union League Club President from 1886 to 1892). For example, Choate turned his address at the dedication of a statue of David Farragut into a dramatic performance of the sayings of famous admirals in the midst of battle. He whispered Nelson's dying words at Trafalgar, and thundered Farragut's declaration at Mobile, "Damn the torpedoes, Captain Drayton. Four bells! Full speed ahead!"[106]

When Choate offered to assist the saddened Harvard student, T.R. said he hoped to get involved in electoral politics. Choate must have been appalled. Like the elder Roosevelt and most other Union League Club members at that time, his idea of politics had far less to do with the grubby tactics of harvesting votes than with

implementing grand ideals as policy. Ward and precinct politics were not part of the world of Choate or, for that matter, most Union League Club members. Nevertheless, young Roosevelt loved going into political clubs and bantering with street politicians and voters. Choate encouraged him to run for the New York State Assembly and offered to help pay his expenses. When Roosevelt did run in 1881, at the age of twenty-two, half the men who signed his nominating petition were Union League Club members. Upon winning that election, Roosevelt wrote Choate, "As I feel that I owe both my nomination and my election more to you than to any other one man, I wish to tell you how I have appreciated both your kind sympathy and the support you have given me. I have taken a somewhat heavy burden of responsibility upon my shoulders, and I regret that I have, of necessity, had so little experience; but at least I shall endeavor to do my work honestly."[107] More experience would come, but sometimes painfully for the opinionated and sometimes impulsive young Roosevelt's friends and admirers.

Choate's encouragement and assistance were matched by T.R.'s other Union League mentor, Elihu Root. Raised a country boy in upstate New York, Root came to the City in the 1860s to attend law school at Columbia. He quickly discovered that he had much to learn. "I perceived in looking around about me that there was a great field of life in New York of which I was ignorant and to which I was unknown," he would write. "I thought it would be useful to fix myself in relation to the life of New York." Considering various ways to enter this new world, he decided, "The best step to take in view of my own feelings, ideas and conceptions of life was to join the Union League Club."[108]

The Club was more than a tutor to the young man: "I came into the Club when I was twenty-three years of age. For the ten years between 1868 and 1878 when I married, this was my home."[109] Root served twice as Club President (1898 to 1899 and 1915 to 1916) and was an important and influential lawyer and public figure, a member of various presidential cabinets and a recipient of the Nobel Prize for Peace.

Elihu Root was a leading legal, diplomatic, and political figure who, like Roosevelt,
was awarded the Nobel Prize for Peace.
(Augustus Vincent Tack)

in perpetual, exuberant motion, while the two older men, Choate and Root, were more cautious and skeptical, as his father had been. "I am extremely fond of him and praise his companionship as well as his advice," Roosevelt said of Root, adding that he especially enjoyed Root's quiet sense of humor.[110]

Despite his lineage and the backing of Choate and Root, when Roosevelt's name was presented for membership in the Union League Club in 1884, he was turned down by the vote of the members. There may have been concerns about his youth (he was only twenty-five) or his combustible temperament, or perhaps his rise seemed too fast. Whatever the reason, the Club's officers made sure his name came up again quickly by interpreting the admissions rules in his favor, and he was elected to membership.

Among Root's and Choate's friends at the Union League Club was a towering Republican with independent convictions from upstate New York, Chester A. Arthur. His lack of enthusiasm for civil service reform lost him appointment as Collector of the Port of New York, but in 1880, Arthur was elected Vice President of the United States. Six months later, President James A. Garfield was assassinated and Arthur was President.

After he backed civil service reform, he became highly regarded at the Union League Club. When poor health kept Arthur from running for election in 1884, the leading Republican candidate was an opportunist from Maine, James G. Blaine. Although Blaine had no support at the Union League Club, young Roosevelt campaigned for him, explaining, "I have been called a reformer but I am a Republican." Roosevelt's decision antagonized the Union League Club circle, but it confirmed that he was in politics for life.[111] The worldly Root and others understood, but many other Union League Club members were appalled that Roosevelt seemed to be sacrificing his moral principles to ambition.

When Roosevelt ran for New York City mayor in 1886, Root organized a rally for him at the Club and gave a rousing speech in which he patched up the wounds of the Blaine incident. Roosevelt lost the election and was appointed to the federal Civil Service Commission, but Root had helped him win acceptance at

Chester A. Arthur
(Eastman Johnson)
Arthur was the first regular member of the Club to serve as President of the United States (1881-84).

Root came to learn what the Club stood for, but the Club was in Theodore Roosevelt's fundamental makeup. He respected clubs in a general way, as institutions that, when managed and led properly, aided society, but he could rebel against their authority. He rebelled against the Union League Club, too, even though his father had been a leading figure there. The young firebrand and his older friends made odd couples. The emotional Roosevelt was

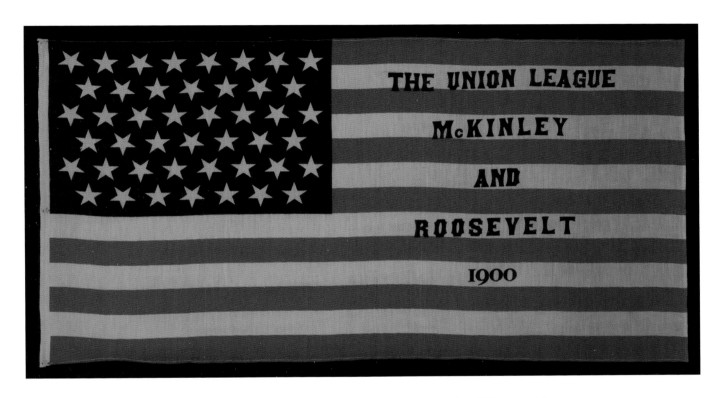

This banner was flown at the Clubhouse during the election in which William McKinley and the forty-two-year-old Roosevelt were elected President and Vice President in 1900.

the Club, which appointed him to the powerful Committee on Political Reform. A few years after the election, Roosevelt wrote a book about New York in which he went out of his way to review the recent history of City clubs. He was especially interested in the ones that he described as having "a politico-social character." The most noted of these clubs, he wrote, was the Union League Club, "alike for its architecture, its political influence, and its important past history."[112]

Roosevelt used the Club fairly frequently, but he was not inclined to mix in a "clubbable" way with other members. A long-time staff member, John McCrae, the "captain" of the Billiard Room, would see Roosevelt race in from the street to the dining room, where he often ate alone while reading a book. In the afternoon, T.R. would come to the Café not for a drink but in search

of companionship and a conversation, which he would usually dominate. Sometimes he would hole up in the Library, the Dining Room Alcove, or a corner of the café to negotiate with a political opponent or encourage an ally, applying the force of his personality in a setting that was fully identified with the Republican Party. When Roosevelt was President of the Board of the New York City Police Commissioners, he held dinners at the Club. The table decorations were tiny *papier-mâché* patrolmen that he would hand out to the waiters to take home to their children.

The Union League Club figures in one of the most colorful stories about T.R. Soon after he was appointed Police Commissioner, he and Jacob A. Riis, a journalist and reformer, undertook a midnight tour of the city, incognito, in order to observe police sloth and corruption. In his memoir, *Making of an American*, Riis (a Danish

President Roosevelt Sits for His Portrait

The story of painting Roosevelt's portrait colorfully encapsulates both the powerful personality of the man known as and the lengths the Union League Club and his friends went in order to be sure a proper representation of its great men was made for the art collection. The artist, George Burroughs Torrey, made a special effort to get his subject right.

When Club member and Secretary of the Treasury Paul Morton commissioned the portrait in 1905, to Torrey's astonishment, Morton insisted that the only way to get T.R. in full character was to irritate him. "Make him mad," Morton instructed Torrey. "You'll get him best that way. Tell him you don't like him, or that New York has no confidence in him. Say anything you think he won't like." Aware that Roosevelt was most comfortable when he paced around, Torrey insisted that Roosevelt sit down.

"No such thing," snapped Roosevelt. "Never sit down." This time was the exception. Roosevelt stewed through four (literal) sittings before Torrey allowed him a look at the portrait. Roosevelt slapped Morton on the back and bellowed, "My boy, you've got Theodore!" Roosevelt later wrote across a corner of a photograph of the painting, "The only successful portrait of me ever painted." [122]

immigrant) recalled that he met up with Roosevelt at the front door of the Union League Club, where they were looked on with suspicion by the Club's night watchmen. Later, they found six policemen sleeping on the job. One, Riis recalled, "was sitting asleep on a butter-tub in the middle of the sidewalk, snoring so that you could hear him across the street, and was inclined to be 'sassy' when aroused and told to go about his duty." Roosevelt ordered the six men to report to headquarters, where he

severely reprimanded them and warned that, next time, they would be fired. [113]

Roosevelt was also hard on saloon keepers who broke the law by keeping their establishments open on Sundays, the only day their blue-collar, mostly immigrant clientele had any time off to relax. As Roosevelt shut down saloons, the mayor was heard to complain that somehow he had a Puritan for his police commissioner. "Principled belligerence" was how one of T.R.'s biographers, Richard Zachs, characterized his personality, but whatever it was called, his moralistic streak eventually cost Roosevelt his Police Commissioner job and sent him off to Washington, where he won national attention. [114]

Roosevelt occasionally lightened up. An elderly waiter in the Club, Seldon Miles, said that once when he served Roosevelt a cup of tea, T.R. leaned over and whispered to him, "Miles, outside there's an officer standing. Give him a drink." [115]

In or out of uniform, T.R. was a soldier, and it was as a Rough Rider in the Spanish-American War that he won his fame. In 2001, Roosevelt was posthumously awarded the Medal of Honor for his actions in Cuba. After his return, Roosevelt ran for New York governor in 1898, and again his mentors were on hand to help. At a mass rally for him at Carnegie Hall, Joseph Choate opened his speech, "I could not stay away from this meeting because I have known Colonel Roosevelt and loved Colonel Roosevelt from his cradle, and I know there is not one drop of blood in his body or one fibre in his being that is not brave, honest, and patriotic." [116]

When Choate was appointed Ambassador to the Court of St. James's a year later, the Union League Club honored him with a large dinner. Choate led off with an outburst of affection for the Union League and its ideals: "What memories the very name of this association calls up! What a school it has been for an Ambassador who shall represent the real America in any country of the world! A school of unconditional loyalty from the beginning. A school of earnest patriotism. A school for the elevation of all that is good and great in the social and political life of America."

At the end of the evening, over cigars and brandy, Root, who presided, introduced the man assigned the honor of offering the last toast. He was the new Governor of New York, whom Root humorously introduced as having "the unknown name of Theodore Roosevelt." At the age of thirty-nine, T.R. was one of the most famous men in the country. Amid a thunder of cheers and applause, Roosevelt arose from his chair and toasted Choate as "the archetype of the kind of American citizenship which this Club prides itself upon having produced." He ended on a deeply personal note: "I myself know well what I owe to Mr. Choate; and I know you will not think that I wander from our subject of this evening when I say that I appreciate to the full the way in which both Mr. Choate and Mr. Root have helped me when I have needed to draw upon all that I could draw upon in the way of intelligence and disinterested interest in the public good."[117]

President Roosevelt

In 1900, soon after he was elected Vice President of the United States under William McKinley, Roosevelt made up his mind to host a dinner to honor J. Pierpont Morgan. One of the few surviving personal links to his father, Morgan had helped him get his start in politics, and they shared many friends and were members of the Union League Club. Yet Morgan was a prominent member of the group Roosevelt called "malefactors of great wealth." Roosevelt's ambivalence is clear in the awkward, forced humor of his explanation of the invitation in a letter to Elihu Root, then Secretary of War: "You see, it represents an effort on my part to become a conservative man, in touch with the influential classes, and I think I deserve encouragement."[118] Held at the Union League Club, the dinner was successful. Nine months later, in September 1901, McKinley was assassinated at the Buffalo World's Fair. Root was the man Roosevelt wanted at his side on the long, somber train ride to Washington.

The complicated relationship between Theodore Roosevelt and the Union League Club did not end when he moved to the White House, and neither did the assistance of Roosevelt's mentors. Upon completing a reform of the Army in 1904, Root resigned as

Hamilton Fish (Club President 1879-1881) was one of three members who served as U.S. Secretary of State by 1905.
(J. Carroll Beckwith)

Secretary of War and returned to New York and his legal practice. "I have missed, and shall miss, Root dreadfully," Roosevelt told his son Theodore. "He has been the ablest, most generous, and most disinterested friend and adviser that any President could hope to have." Root had stood before the members of the Union League Club and defended Roosevelt's criticisms of business, which were not at all popular among most Republicans. In his letter to his son, Roosevelt complimented Root for that speech, "in which he said in most effective fashion the very things I should have liked him to say; and his words, moreover, carried weight as the words

UNITED STATES SENATE.
WASHINGTON.

March 29, 1913.

Dear Sir:

I have received your letter of March 25th and I shall be
glad to have you say to the boys in your club that President
Grant is a good example of real strength. He was a quiet, self-
controlled, considerate, and kindly man. He never blustered or
raged or threatened or talked loudly and harshly; but he was
one of the strongest of men. He had inflexible resolution,
great tenacity of purpose. He never gave up anything that he
undertook. He could not be turned aside. He was a terrible
fighter. He commanded great armies; he won great victories;
but he never hated anybody, never tried to injure anybody. He
had no spitefulness or meanness or smallness in his disposition.
He was kindly and gentle in his family. He was simple, and truth-
ful, and honest, and forgiving. He was faithful to his friends.
He loved his country. He had sympathy for every one who was in
trouble or suffering. If you see a boy who swaggers and boasts
and talks loud; who is coarse and boorish and who is mean and
tricky, remember that he is not like the great, strong Grant,
who commanded armies and won victories and had great honor and
fame over all the world. But he is like the camp followers who
skulked when there was danger and talked loud when there was
safety.

Very truly yours,

Elihu Root

Mr. J. E. Boos, Superintendent,
Public Bath No. 3,
Albany, New York.

o/

"He was one of the strongest of men," U.S. Senator Elihu Root
said of Ulysses S. Grant in this deeply felt letter.
Generous gift of Marsha Malinowski on the occasion
of the 150th Anniversary of the Club.

Charles Evans Hughes (Club President 1917-1919)
(George Burroughs Torrey)
Hughes won the 1916 Republican
Presidential nomination over two other Club members.

of no other man at this time addressing such an audience could have done."[119] What Root had said at the Club was this: "President Roosevelt is conservative."[120] On another occasion at the Club, Root insisted that Roosevelt was not anti-business and pro-labor but "the greatest conservative force for the protection of property and our institutions in the City of Washington."[121] Roosevelt easily won the 1904 election and immediately recalled Root to Washington as Secretary of State, a position previously held by two other Presidents of the Union League Club, William Evarts (1882 to 1885) and Hamilton Fish (1897 to 1881).

Roosevelt declined to run for election in 1908 and headed off to Africa on a hunting expedition, but four years later, he upset his mentors and the entire Republican Party by challenging President William Howard Taft, his one-time protégé, for the Republican nomination at the convention. When Taft won, Roosevelt blamed Root, who was the party chairman, and (forgetting his "I am a Republican" rule) ran on the third-party Progressive "Bull Moose" ticket. This ensured that Taft was only the third Republican to lose a presidential campaign in over half a century. These events badly scarred Roosevelt's relations with Root, Taft, and the Union League Club.

At the time of the 1916 election, Root was serving his second term as Club President. He and Choate helped choreograph a try at a public reconciliation between Taft and Roosevelt, both Union League Club members, during a reception at the Club for

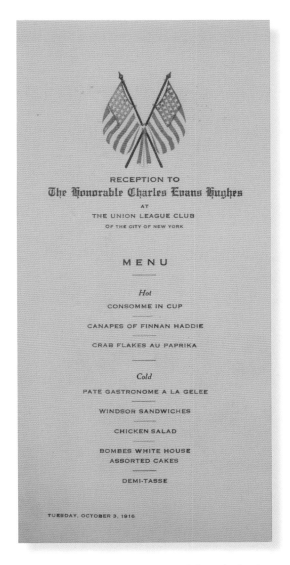

RECEPTION TO
The Honorable Charles Evans Hughes
AT
THE UNION LEAGUE CLUB
OF THE CITY OF NEW YORK

MENU

Hot
CONSOMME IN CUP

CANAPES OF FINNAN HADDIE

CRAB FLAKES AU PAPRIKA

Cold
PATE GASTRONOME A LA GELEE

WINDSOR SANDWICHES

CHICKEN SALAD

BOMBES WHITE HOUSE
ASSORTED CAKES

DEMI-TASSE

TUESDAY, OCTOBER 3, 1916

"I was only the side show," Hughes said about this luncheon at the Club a month before the 1916 election.

the Republican candidate for President, Charles Evans Hughes, also a Club member and Club President from 1917 to 1919.

Roosevelt made clear his own feelings about the event when he described it in terms more suited to the Bad Lands: "It was one of those friendly affairs where each side, before entering the meeting place, made sure its hardware was in working order." After elaborate preparations, the two men were separately led into an elevator at the Club and, well out of the view of the press, briefly greeted each other. "We shook hands with a Howdy Do and that was all," Taft wrote his wife. Hughes' comment was apt: "I was only the side show."[123] This momentary era of good feelings between the two Republican Presidents was the subject of newspaper headlines and defused the public tension, but it did not win the election for Charles Evans Hughes.

Discouraged, sick with ailments and grief for a son killed in the world war that he supported, Roosevelt died in 1919 in his sixty-first year. Joseph Choate predeceased him in 1917, leaving Elihu Root to eulogize Roosevelt with feeling and generosity at a memorial gathering: "So many of us loved him! The mystic chords of memory draw the hearts of so many of us back to that life so magnanimous, so kindly, so affectionate, so appealing to the best in all our natures, so full of genuine interest in our fortunes, so appreciative of what was good in us, so kindly and considerate in our failings! We love him!"[124]

The Union League Club, 1863–2013

The Buffalo Soldiers and the Harlem Hellfighters

At the time Roosevelt and Taft were making a semblance of a personal truce in the Fall of 1916, Americans were focusing on a much larger issue: should the country enter the war in Europe? Of all major nations, only the United States remained neutral. As Germany engaged in a series of provocative acts against Americans, President Woodrow Wilson ran for a second term on a platform headed by the statement, "He kept us out of war." It pleased many Democrats and western and rural Republicans, but not the Union League Club. When 125,000 men and women marched up Fifth Avenue in the pro-intervention Preparedness Parade in May 1916, many Club members joined their ranks or stood outside the Clubhouse and cheered them. The *Yearbook* called it, "The greatest parade in the history of our country."[125]

Opposite: *World War I "Buffalo Soldiers" Regimental Standard*

The Club enthusiastically supported Preparedness and the Allies in World War I.

All three candidates for the Republican nomination—New York Governor Charles S. Whitman, Senator Elihu Root, and Charles Evans Hughes—were Club members. A former New York Governor, Secretary of State, and Supreme Court Justice, Hughes won at the convention. Many Club members marched in an election eve torchlight parade for Hughes through the streets of Manhattan, but the next day, he narrowly lost the election. Wilson's neutrality policy wavered early in 1917 as Germany engaged in indiscriminate submarine warfare and incited a small war on the Mexican-American border. "Nothing could be more dramatic than the change that came over the United States in the first three months of the year 1917," said Henry P. Davison (Club President, 1920). "The weary period of inaction was drawing to its end. The signs were no longer to be misread. Honor had been stretched to its last shred of endurance and continued peace, it was plain, could only be had at the price of shame."[126]

In late March (to quote Hughes' biographer) "600 Republicans met at the Union League Club behind closed doors and virtually declared war on Germany ahead of the government."[127] The featured speakers were Theodore Roosevelt, Joseph Choate, and

Henry P. Davison (Club President 1920)
Davison headed the wartime activities
of "the Greatest Mother in the World," the American Red Cross.
(Sidney Dickinson)

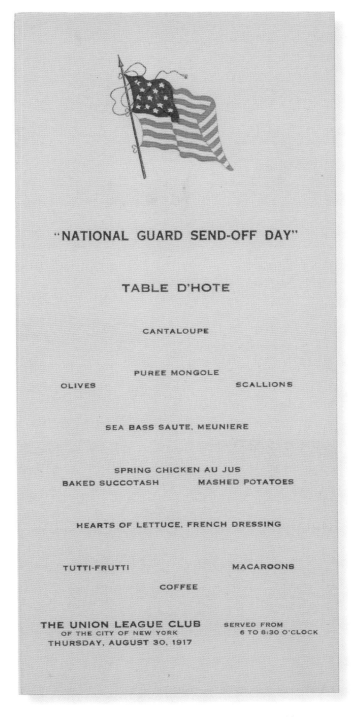

"NATIONAL GUARD SEND-OFF DAY"

TABLE D'HOTE

CANTALOUPE

PUREE MONGOLE

OLIVES   SCALLIONS

SEA BASS SAUTE, MEUNIERE

SPRING CHICKEN AU JUS
BAKED SUCCOTASH   MASHED POTATOES

HEARTS OF LETTUCE, FRENCH DRESSING

TUTTI-FRUTTI   MACAROONS

COFFEE

THE UNION LEAGUE CLUB   SERVED FROM
OF THE CITY OF NEW YORK   6 TO 8:30 O'CLOCK
THURSDAY, AUGUST 30, 1917

The scope of the Club's public activities during the World Wars
is indicated by this and other menus and event programs in its collection.

Elihu Root (making the final joint appearance in their long relationship), with Hughes, who had been elected the Club's President after the election. The men were a dramatic contrast: the furious Roosevelt, the avuncular Choate, the intense Root, and the regal Hughes, with his Edwardian beard and formality. To the members and to the nation, these men *were* the Union League Club. The theme for the evening was established by the one speaker who had fought in war. "War now exists by act of Germany," Roosevelt thundered. "There is no question about 'going to war.' Germany is already at war with us."

Hughes echoed him: "The only question for us to decide is whether we shall make war nobly or ignobly."[128]

Root announced, "It is either war or submission to oppression."[129] Eighty-six-year-old Joseph Choate waved the battle flag of the Union League Club's founders:

"I am often asked today, What can we do; what can we mere citizens do, when our Government is doing nothing or doing so little; what can we do for our country? Let me tell you what they did. . . . By the founding of this Club, and the appeals of its members in public and in private, the sentiment of the City was changed, or rather, the loyal sentiment overrode and suppressed the disloyal sentiment that had previously prevailed. They raised and equipped two regiments for the service of their country, which immediately entered that service."[130]

Hearing all this, Roosevelt exclaimed, "My, how the atmosphere has changed!"[131]

Later that evening, in the Club bar, T.R. begged Choate and Root to persuade Wilson to grant him an army commission. He wished to die with honor on French soil. "Theodore," joked Root, "if you can convince Wilson of that, I am sure he will give you a commission."[132]

On April 6, Wilson and Congress declared war. Choate died in May. Root headed a government mission to St. Petersburg to feel out the Bolsheviks, who refused to meet with him. Hughes was named by Governor Whitman to head the city's Draft Appeals Board (in this war, the military draft inspired no riots, only complaints). As for Roosevelt, he did not receive his commission. Bitter and gravely ill, he rapidly wore down, dying in 1919.

The Early Fight for Civil Rights

The Club was represented in many regiments, but two of them attracted special attention because they were reminiscent of the Union League Club's activities in the Civil War. The two regiments are represented by a stand of colors displayed in a case in the Clubhouse. These are the colors of the 367th Infantry Regiment, one of the segregated "colored" units in the Ninety-Second

Col. James A. Moss, commander of "The Buffalo Soldiers" 367th Regiment of Infantry. The Club presented the 367th its colors on March 23, 1918.

Infantry Division that were sometimes called "Buffalo Soldiers" (because a buffalo was sometimes on their colors).

Theodore Roosevelt addressed the 367th when it was in training, before it was shipped to France. It was still in combat on the last day of the war, November 11, 1918.

While the service of the 367th was noteworthy, at least as significant was another predominately black regiment with Union

On the Home Front

When America eventually went to war, it was in a rush of both ferocity and humanity unmatched since the Civil War. The Club then had 1,900 members, and 1,701 of them signed a declaration of agreement that contained the familiar words, "absolute loyalty to the government of the United States." The Club faced the challenge expressed in a note in the *Yearbook*: "The question uppermost in the minds of the members seemed to be how to make the Club of greatest service to the nation during its struggle with the Hun."[133]

As the Union League Club members rushed to volunteer for the military and other public service organizations, the Club displayed a wartime service banner on the building alongside an illuminated electric American flag. By January 1, 1918, more than 140 Club members were serving in the war in some capacity, including officials of the government, foreign service, or the American Red Cross. Among the 103 men in military uniform were famous names such as Major Ulysses S. Grant III (Elihu Root's son-in-law) and Brigadier General Cornelius Vanderbilt III, commanding an infantry brigade. Theodore Roosevelt and seven other members lost sons in the war.

At the Clubhouse, Liberty Bonds were sold from a booth and the Club sponsored or co-sponsored a total of twenty-seven patriotic or military events, including open houses, receptions, rallies, and soldiers' parades up Fifth Avenue watched by hundreds of members and their families in the Club's reviewing stand. As the City was flooded by men in uniform, the Club leased the former Princeton Club, near Gramercy Park, and converted it into an officer's billet called the Union League Club Unit. The original allotment of seventy beds was quickly increased to eighty-five, and 1,147 officers were cared for in May 1918 alone. Several members acquired a motorboat they named *Union League Club* to serve as a launch between the City and a sailors' and soldiers' convalescent home on an island in Lower New York Bay.

Other members participated in the war effort by expressing their patriotic concerns at Club meetings. At one time or another, members proposed that the Club prohibit Germans from entering the Clubhouse and bar conversations in German there, that the state pass a law banning the teaching of German in public schools, and that a fund be established to publish patriotic pamphlets "not only in English but in Yiddish and other languages."[134] One especially assiduous believer in "loyalism," Archibald Stevenson, headed Club committees seeking out German sympathizers and, after the armistice, led hunts for radicals and communists.

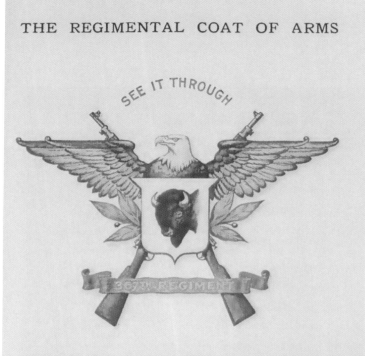

THE REGIMENTAL COAT OF ARMS

SEE IT THROUGH

367TH REGIMENT

The EAGLE symbolizes the United States of America.

The CROSSED RIFLES mean Infantry.

The BUFFALO HEAD signifies colored soldier, because in frontier days the Indians used to call our colored soldiers "Buffalo Soldiers," because in color they were black or brown like the Buffalo, and like the Buffalo they were good fighters, as the Indians had learned from experience.

The REGIMENTAL MOTTO, "See It Through,' expresses the spirit, the soul of the Regiment.

The LAUREL LEAVES typify victory,—the victory that the Regiment will always bend every effort to achieve, and for which it will willingly make every sacrifice.

The spirit of the Buffalo Soldiers tradition is clear in the regimental coat of arms of one of the Union League Club's "colored" regiments, the 367th, which the Union League Club honored and presented with colors.

League Club connections. This was the all-volunteer Fifteenth Regiment (Colored) in the New York National Guard, later renamed the 369th Infantry Regiment and assigned to the French Army. Few if any other U.S. regiments were in combat for a longer period of time, 191 days, or had a higher casualty rate (over 40 percent) or earned more medals—or played such an important role in the history of music.

The commander of the Fifteenth was Union League Club member, William L. Hayward. Born and raised in a dusty frontier town, Nebraska City, Nebraska, Will Hayward starred on the University of Nebraska football team, was president of his class, earned a law degree, and gained an army commission in a militia unit called the Pershing Rifles that was trained by a young lieutenant, John J. Pershing. After graduation, Hayward volunteered for the Spanish-American War and spent two years in Cuba and the Philippines. The man was at heart an adventurer. His granddaughter, Brooke Hayward (daughter of his son Leland Hayward, a well-known film and stage producer), wrote of his "old ache, a wildness and lust for adventure, never quite satisfied by the perimeters of civilization."

On the outlook for more action, the intense, ambitious Hayward returned home as a colonel in the Nebraska National Guard, practiced law, became the Republican state party chairman, and ran the western portion of William Howard Taft's victorious 1908 presidential campaign against Nebraskan William Jennings Bryan. After losing a race for Congress, Hayward revived his spirits with a honeymoon trip around the world with his first wife before moving to New York, where political allies helped him gain appointment as Assistant District Attorney. In 1910, Will Hayward joined the Union League Club.

District Attorney Charles S. Whitman was also a Club member and had served as Secretary. Like Hayward, Whitman was charismatic, creative, moralistic, and very ambitious. The case that made his reputation was the prosecution of a New York police lieutenant, Charles Becker, for arranging the murder of a small-time crook, Herman Rosenthal, who was about to go to Whitman to file corruption charges against Becker. Becker was found guilty of first-degree murder and sentenced to death. By then, Whitman had been elected Governor (Hayward was his campaign manager). When Becker pled for clemency, Whitman, refusing to recuse himself, turned him down. After Becker was electrocuted in 1915, his family attempted to attach to his coffin a statement accusing Whitman of murder. Becker is the only New York police officer ever to be executed. This spectacular case remains controversial, with stubborn claims that Becker was framed.[135]

Riding a "Whitman for President" boomlet, Whitman finished third behind his fellow Union League Club members, Charles Evans Hughes and Elihu Root, at the 1916 Republican National Convention and delivered the speech nominating Hughes.

By that time, New York was involved in a conflict on a distant border that would soon involve Will Hayward. In the spring of 1916, a Mexican bandit, Pancho Villa, led a violent incursion into New Mexico, killing several American citizens amid reports that he was a tool in a German plot to distract the United States from entering the war in Europe. The government undertook an undeclared war to corral Villa, called the Mexican Punitive Expedition. The War Department ordered New York State to send a National Guard division to participate. This left New York without any National Guard units at home. Obliged to form a new regiment, Whitman picked up on an idea suggested by Edwin Horne of Brooklyn (the grandfather of the singer Lena Horne) and formed a new "colored regiment," the Fifteenth. The man he appointed as its commanding officer was his aide, the former colonel in the Nebraska National Guard, William Hayward. Once again a Union League Club member would march at the head of a black regiment. This regiment was nationally known as "The Harlem Hellfighters."

The Club's history of activity favorable to African Americans dated back to its founders' support of Abraham Lincoln and creation of Civil War Colored Regiments. In 1903, when President Theodore Roosevelt invited Booker T. Washington, the respected black educator, to dinner in the White House, the response in the

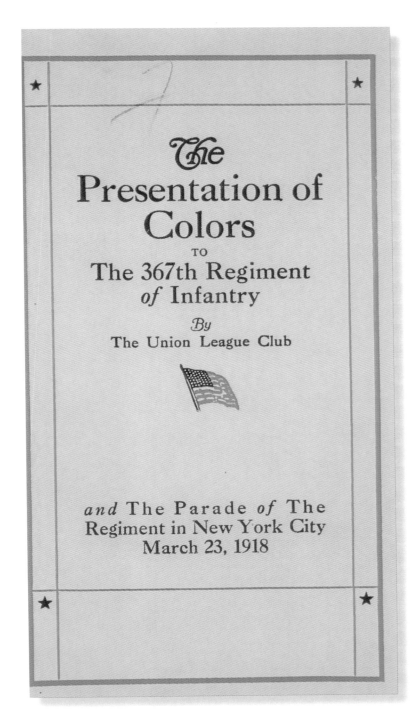

After the 367th received its colors, the Buffalo Soldiers embarked for France arriving in June 1918. The regiment had a notable record, including the award by France of the Croix de Guerre.

South was so furious that Roosevelt felt obliged to back down on his promise to appoint black officials and press for black suffrage.

In protest, the Union League Club passed a resolution calling on Congress to guarantee the right to vote for African Americans. Club members volunteered in civil rights organizations, one serving on the board of the National Association for the Advancement of Colored People. When the Ku Klux Klan was riding high in the 1920s, Elihu Root publicly attacked it as "narrow-minded men who have been left behind in the general development of the moral nature of our people, against a progress that they dislike."[136]

All this was noticed by African Americans. When the *Baltimore Afro-American* reported the Club's move into its new clubhouse in 1931, the story ran under the headline, "The Union League, Anti-Slavery Champion, Gets a New Clubhouse."[137]

Colonel Hayward in Command

Despite its grand aims, the Fifteenth Regiment in its first weeks had only one staff member, Colonel Will Hayward, moonlighting from his government job and recruiting troops out of a Harlem cigar store. His flamboyant nature was up to the challenge. "The recruiting of a regiment is to a considerable degree a question of showmanship," he told Major Arthur Little, his second in command who later wrote a history of the Fifteenth, *From Harlem to the Rhine*. Little appreciated Hayward's aptitude for being "brilliant, aggressive, good-natured, cynical, humorous, winning, and forceful in every way for which he was famous."[138]

Once the government imposed the draft, the regiment reached full strength but left Hayward with the problem of finding a place and means to conduct drills. Training began in the Harlem streets with broomsticks, and moved to a dance hall with rifles that Hayward acquired by claiming that he was forming a shooting club. In early October 1916, Hayward and his officers marched the regiment down to the Union League Clubhouse, where Governor Whitman presented them with their regimental colors.

Some officers were black, but black or white, very few had any military experience except for Hayward and Little, a middle-aged Army reserve officer. One of the black officers was a popular Ziegfeld Follies comedian named Bert Williams, another was a Harvard educated lawyer named Napoleon Bonaparte Marshall who was the first African American to offer to enlist after the ocean liner *Lusitania* was sunk by a German torpedo in 1915.

The bandleader was also African American, Lieutenant James Reese Europe, who was one of the most famous, successful popular musicians in America. Europe was the composer and conductor who took ragtime and transformed it into jazz. The dance impresarios Vernon and Irene Castle said they would perform with no other orchestra than Jim Europe's. Europe joined the Fifteenth because Hayward heard him play and announced that he wanted the best band he could find. When the band needed a little reinforcing, Hayward raised some funds and sent Europe to Puerto Rico to recruit clarinet and saxophone players.

After several weeks of training at army camps in upstate New York and South Carolina (where racial tensions almost erupted in violence), the Fifteenth returned to the City only to find themselves shut out of a grand review for the Army's Forty-Second Division, known as the Rainbow Division. "Black was not one of the colors of the rainbow," Hayward commented.[139] He promised to march up Fifth Avenue when the Fifteenth returned home from the war.

When the Union League Club served a dinner to the regiment, the white soldiers and officers were received in the Clubhouse by the Club's officers and members, and the black soldiers were sent to a hotel in Harlem, where one of the Club's longtime black staff members, Joseph Queenan, served as toastmaster. One Club member did come up and express a few words of welcome.[140]

With its ship regularly breaking down, the Fifteenth Regiment needed four tries before it reached France in late 1917. Once there, the regiment was assigned to the French Army to provide support for white regiments. In an article after the war, Hayward wrote that the Fifteenth "was the street urchin of New York National Guard regiments that now found itself the black orphan of the Army, left on the door-step of the French."[141] He asked his former training officer, Pershing, commander of U.S. forces in Europe, if a home could be found in the American army. The answer was another disappointment. In a footnote in his memoirs, Pershing wrote vaguely that he had "made application" to see if any of his generals would agree to take them, "but to no purpose and these regiments remained with the French to the end."[142]

Their luck turned. In April, the Fifteenth was fully absorbed into the French Fourth Army and renamed the 369th Regiment d'Infanterie, U.S. The Army's commander, General Henri Gouraud, known as "the Lion of the Argonne," had lost an arm at Gallipoli but was in full command. Having served with Algerian troops for many years, he and his officers were not hamstrung by racial prejudice. Following his first meeting with this grandiose character, Hayward wrote, "I understood at the end of our interview the French phrase, 'The mere sight of him made men brave.'" Gouraud gave him money to distribute to the families of battle casualties, telling Hayward, "It is only a little, but the Americans have done such wonderful things for our unfortunate people."[143]

Jim Europe's jazz band, meanwhile, was playing around France. Noble Sissle, Europe's chief assistant, looked back on the moment when the band launched into "Memphis Blues" at one of its first concerts. "The audience could stand it no longer. The 'jazz germ' hit them and it seemed to find the vital spot loosening all muscles and causing what is known in America as an 'eagle rocking it.' . . . I was forced to say that this is just what France needs at this critical time."[144] A Union League Club member, Hayward could accurately claim that he was in command of a foreign mission for America's music.

In Battle

Will Hayward got his war, and he performed with Rooseveltian bravado. At one time or another, he was heard to declare, "My men never retire; they go forward or they die," and "The first thing I knew there was nothing between the German army and Paris except my regiment," and "No German ever got into a trench with my regiment who didn't stay there or go back with the brand of my boys on them."[145] Besides providing a warrior's justification for the regiment's "Hellfighters" nickname, his boasts approximated the truth. By the end of the war, the 369th suffered more than 1,500 casualties, with 367 dead. The regiment's officers and the men were awarded more than 150 medals. Hayward, who won three medals, was said to have ripped the bird colonel eagles off his uniform, grabbed a rifle, leapt out of the trench, and led his men through artillery fire. Privates Henry Johnson and Needham Roberts put a German raiding party to rout and were awarded the Croix de Guerre. (In 2003, President George W. Bush awarded Johnson a posthumous Distinguished Cross, presenting it to his son, who was one of the Tuskegee Airmen of World War II.)

The 369th worked its way across France, and in the second Battle of the Marne, helped block a German breakthrough toward Paris. On Armistice Day, November 11, Allied Forces began a race to the Rhine. Hayward believed he was first to arrive. He told Little, "I climbed down the bank, and I scooped up some of the water in my hands, and I drank it as I breathed a prayer of thanksgiving. And I said to those officers who were with me—Little, I said to them in a kind of boastful way—that I felt as if neither DeSoto, nor Drake, nor Frobisher, nor even Columbus had anything on me."[146]

The Fifteenth Regiment (Colored) returned to New York in February 1919 and it finally got its parade up Fifth Avenue, marching behind James Reese Europe and his band, pausing at Thirty-Ninth Street to exchange salutes with members of the Union League Club. A month later, the 367th U.S. Infantry, "the Buffalo Soldiers," marched to the Clubhouse and returned the regimental colors that Governor Whitman had presented to them before they embarked for Europe. The message sent to the Club by a member who was an officer of the 367th, Hulbert D. Bassett, indicates the intense emotions of these occasions. The regiment was returning those colors to the Union League, he wrote, "in order that they may be an uplift to the present and coming generations, as they have been to us in field and combat, as well as bring additional luster to your splendid organization in its patriotic purposes and aims."[147] This is the stand of colors displayed in the case in the Club's Members Lounge.

The men of the war returned to peacetime with mixed success. Charles S. Whitman lost the 1918 gubernatorial election to Democrat Al Smith, founded a law firm, was defeated for the presidential nomination in 1924, and then lost a race for his old job, District Attorney. For a few years, Whitman chaired the Club's Committee on Public Affairs (the former Committee on Political Reform).

Will Hayward came home from France in 1919 and married Maisie Plant, the young widow of one of the country's richest men, Morton Plant. (Plant was said to have sold his house on Fifth Avenue to the jeweler Cartier in exchange for a necklace, valued at $1 million, that he presented to Maisie.) After several years as United States Attorney for the Southern District of New York, he ran for the Republican nomination for Governor in 1924. His platform featured an energetic criticism of anyone who was tepid about enforcing the Volstead Act. "No law is too good or important to be changed if it is changed by orderly processes of a free people, operating under their own Constitution," Hayward declared. "But no man or woman, however, is too good to obey that law as long as it is on the statute books."[148] Ironically, when this T.R.-style moralist ran for the Republican nomination for Governor, he was beaten by T.R.'s oldest son, Theodore.

Hayward soon retired from public life, and, like Roosevelt before him, went big game hunting. He brought home trophies for the Museum of Natural History and live polar bears for the Bronx and Prospect Park zoos. His last years were spent living in comfort in New York, Newport, and Palm Beach. At Will Hayward's funeral in 1944, the pallbearers were officers of the Hellfighters, and the guard of honor consisted of sixty of the black soldiers he had commanded in the Fifteenth Regiment.

Plaque recognizing the service of Club members who served in World War I.

Honorary Members 1894–1927

Honorary Member	Elected to Honorary Membership	Admitted to Regular Membership (if applicable)	Notable Achievements
Charles H. Parkhurst	November 8, 1894		Reverend for the Presbyterian Church and President of the Society for the Prevention of Crime
William McKinley	November 12, 1896		President of the United States
Nelson A. Miles	April 9, 1896	1892	Lieutenant General, United States Army
Horace Porter	January 13, 1898	1872	Union League Club President 1893–1897 Brigadier General, United States Army, Ambassador Extraordinary and Minister Plenipotentiary to France
Thomas C. Acton	February 10, 1898	1864	Founder of the Society for the Prevention of the Cruelty to Animals Commissioner, New York City Police Department
George Dewey	May 12, 1898		Admiral, United States Navy
Elihu Root	1900	1868	Union League Club President 1898–1899 and 1915–1916 Secretary of War of the United States
Grenville M. Dodge	March 14, 1901	1882	Major General, United States Volunteers
Theodore Roosevelt	January 9, 1902	1884	President of the United States
Joseph H. Choate	September 10, 1903	1867	Union League Club President 1873-1876 Ambassador Extraordinary and Minister Plenipotentiary to Great Britain
John Hay	April 14, 1904		Secretary of State of the United States
William H. Taft	March 11, 1909		President of the United States
Charles E. Hughes	1910	1907	Union League Club President 1917–1919 United States Supreme Court Chief Justice, United States Secretary of State, Governor of New York
Cornelius N. Bliss	February 9, 1911	1897	Union League Club President 1902–1906 United States Secretary of the Interior
Andrew D. White	October 9, 1913		Ambassador Extraordinary and Minister Plenipotentiary to the German Empire
Anson G. McCook	November 9, 1916		General, United States Army
John J. Pershing	1919		General of the Armies of the United States
William Sowden Sims	May 19, 1919		Rear Admiral, United States Navy
Leonard W. Wood	April 10, 1919		Major General, United States Army
Warren G. Harding	March 10, 1921		President of the United States
Calvin Coolidge	March 10, 1921		President of the United States
Charles Gates Dawes	1924		Vice President of the United States, Ambassador Extraordinary and Minister Plenipotentiary to Great Britain
Andrew W. Mellon	1927	1897	United States Secretary of the Treasury
Peyton C. March	1927		General, United States Army
Robert Lee Bullard	1927		Major General, United States Army
James G. Harbord	1927		Major General, United States Army
Hugh Rodman	1927		Rear Admiral, United States Navy
Joseph R. Strauss	1927		Rear Admiral, United States Navy
Henry B. Wilson	1927		Rear Admiral, United States Navy
Frederic R. Harris	1927		Rear Admiral, United States Navy
Leigh C. Palmer	1927		Rear Admiral, United States Navy
John A. Lejeune	1927		Major General, Commandant of the United States Marine Corps
Tasker H. Bliss	May 12, 1927		Major General, United States Army
George W. Goethals	May 12, 1927		Major General, United States Army
Albert Parker Niblack	May 12, 1927		Rear Admiral, United States Navy
Francis Hunter Ligget	May 12, 1927		Major General, United States Army

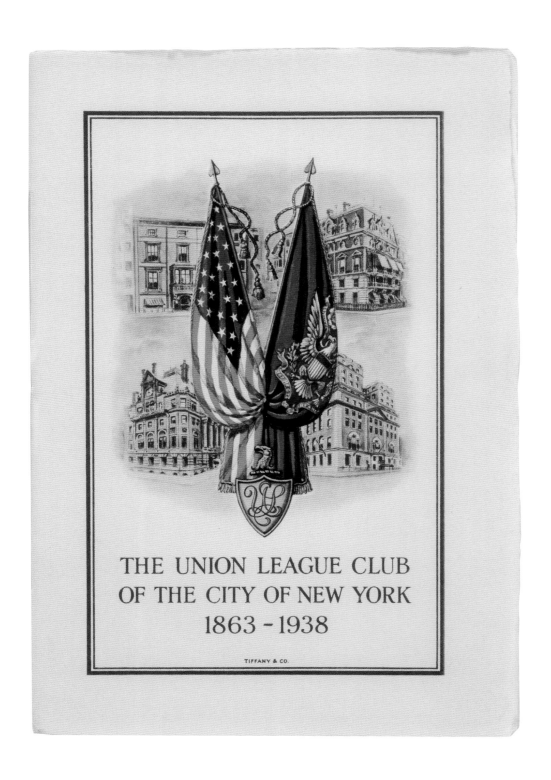

THE UNION LEAGUE CLUB
OF THE CITY OF NEW YORK
1863 – 1938

TIFFANY & CO.

Between the Wars

The largest American public health initiative since the United States Sanitary Commission was the mobilization of the American Red Cross during World War I. After Henry W. Bellows was unsuccessful in persuading the International Red Cross to merge with the Sanitary Commission, the Commission ceased operations in 1877. Four years later, Clara Barton founded the American Red Cross. In 1916, the Red Cross had 107 chapters, 16,000 members, and twenty five paid staff who concentrated on public health nursing and teaching first aid and swimming safety. When America entered the World War, another Union League Club member, Henry Pomeroy Davison (Club President, 1920), transformed the American Red Cross in a matter of weeks into an altogether different institution.

Opposite: Union League Club Colors and Clubhouses, 75th Anniversary

Another vigorous visionary in the mold of the Club's founders and Theodore Roosevelt, Davison was the son of a rural Pennsylvania farm-tools dealer. Opting out of attending college when Harvard declined to give him a scholarship, he found a job in a bank in Bridgeport, Connecticut, where he won the good favor of the showman P.T. Barnum, one of the stockholders, who helped him gain a position as a teller in a New York bank. Davison attracted attention when he foiled an attempted robbery by handing over the money in $1 bills while shouting the count so loudly that his colleagues caught on to the crime and called the police. His skills and confidence caught the attention of George F. Baker, head of the First National Bank (and the Club's longtime Treasurer) and J. Pierpont Morgan. During the 1907 bank panic, Davison and his committees sometimes met at the Union League Club.

"The commanding general over all the other forces in the field," was how he was characterized by his partner Thomas W. Lamont, who explained, "He reconciled differences of view, calmed the uneasy and anxious; he inspired the timid, sometimes disciplined the cowardly, but with it all his courage never flagged, his industry was unceasing, and his good temper never failed him."[149] Davison rose to be a leading partner at J.P. Morgan & Co., where Pierpont Morgan was rumored to have declared, "I always believe everything Mr. Davison tells me."[150]

Davison thought big and acted extravagantly—hunting elephants, building a Long Island estate at a place called Peacock Point, and hosting large parties. Taking charge of the Red Cross War Council in 1917, Davison quickly got to work on what he called, in his book about the Red Cross effort, "massing the forces of mercy."[151] The first step was to raise $100 million (more than $1.2 billion today). The American Red Cross offered all types of assistance—including food, clothing, medical services, hospitality, and recreation—to the military and civilians in the fifty-eight hospitals it ran in Europe. When the influenza pandemic spread, the Red Cross served as a public health agency. In Russia, members of the Red Cross mission dodged bullets in the streets in order to feed and clothe Americans, among others, and ameliorate the misery of political prisoners in Bolshevik prisons. In Italy, the Red Cross cared for a total of 155,000 children. At the end of the war, the American Red Cross had 100,000 volunteers and had raised more than $400 million and spent $273 million. Davison described the Red Cross as "the applied humanity of its community. It represents the organized forces of friendliness and it applies them in ways as varied and as colorful as human need." Others called the Red Cross "The Greatest Mother in the World."[152]

The work was relentless, varied, and exceedingly challenging for the thousands of volunteers, who also included Union League Club members Harvey Gibson, Samuel Green, Frederick P. Small, Cornelius Bliss, Jr., James G. Blaine, Jr., and William Boyce Thompson.

Davison went on to chair the International Red Cross for a year before returning to New York and J.P. Morgan & Co. In 1920, the members of the Union League Club elected him their President. Within a year, he was obliged to resign because of a brain tumor, and he died in 1922.

Utopian Dreams

The return to peace was sudden and, for many people, unsettling. In a speech he gave at Columbia University at the invitation of Union League Club member and Columbia President Nicholas Murray Butler, Club President Charles Evans Hughes expressed concern about the country's post-war direction. He hoped America would return to normal: "We are unworthy of our victory if we look forward with timidity. This is the hour and power of light, not of darkness." But he worried about Americans' tendency to lose themselves in what he called "dreams of immediate utopias." [153]

Elihu Root shared this concern. He feared that Americans were making the double mistake of attempting to create two Utopian dreams. One was President Wilson's proposal to join the League of Nations without carefully limiting the conditions of membership, including the League's authority over American laws and institutions. While many Republicans were isolationists who opposed the League, Root, Hughes, and others in the Union League Club group believed that membership was worthwhile so long as the

One of the gems of the Club's large clock collection is this handsome Art Deco design in the Main Bar.

United States retained its historic independence. The issue became moot when Congress rejected Wilson's plan.

The second "dream" that bothered Root was Prohibition—the national policy, imposed by the proposed new Eighteenth Amendment to the Constitution, of banning the manufacture, sale, and imbibing of alcoholic beverages. Proposed and passed by his fellow Republicans, Prohibition was an administrative burden. Between passage of the Amendment in January 1919 and when it went into effect a year later, private clubs across America sold off their liquor and ordered members to clear all spirits from their private lockers. The law was not always strictly enforced in big cities, yet scandal appears to have stayed away from the Union League's door until the end of Prohibition, which Root and other Union League members helped bring about. Beyond its local, practical burdens, "the noble experiment" ran contrary to Root's and many others' understanding of America and freedom. He told a friend, "Prohibition is as much 'a noble experiment' as the Spanish Inquisition—it is the same idea as forcing people to conduct their lives as you want them to."[154]

"The Great Purposes of Our Country"

Should controversial public issues even be raised in the Club? The founders believed the Union League Club was just the place for debate about large political and social issues. In 1920, the Committee on Political Reform agreed. "In no large and influential organization could it reasonably be expected to find all members of one mind and of uniform views," Committee chairman William D. Guthrie stated in the committee's annual report in 1921, "Indeed, it is ever by the friction of differing and conflicting minds that progress is made and wise conclusions are reached."[155] Elihu Root did not disagree with this view of the Club's role in American life. In the speech he gave at his eightieth birthday party at the Club in February 1925, with his usual vigor and clarity, he laid out his convictions about what made the Club distinctive:

"This Club does not study questions of government scientifically, as many organizations do in these days; it is not a Club of critics, it is a Club of actors in life—and the difference between the two is very great. The observer in the attitude of a critic differs widely from an actor in the attitude of strong desire to accomplish purposes. This institution is an institution composed of actors, not theorists, not students, not scientific enquirers, but men engaged in the work of life, in the attitude of the doer rather than the critic, binding themselves together for the more efficient doing of the things that are necessary to accomplish the great purposes of our country, of our free government."

Root assured his fellow members that the world was a better place than in the past. More people cared more about the general welfare and were doing more to improve it. Elections were more honest, and so were public officials. And he was pleased to say that America was a more tolerant place than ever.[156]

The new clubhouse bar was built while members worked to repeal Prohibition, which Elihu Root called "as much 'a noble experiment' as the Spanish Inquisition."

Herbert Hoover
(George Burroughs Torrey, 1929)

The Alamagoozlum Cocktail

The new bar opened for business on Monday, December 7, 1933, after passage of the Twenty-First Amendment repealed Prohibition. By some accounts, the first libation served that day was an exotic, spicy drink called the Alamagoozlum Cocktail that was said to have been invented by J. Pierpont Morgan. Will Irwin wrote of it in his history of the Club, "Those who have tasted this ambrosia compare its flavor to the first caress of a young love and its effect to the wallop of an Old Man Kangaroo." Here is the recipe as reported in a mixer's guide.[165]

The Alamagoozlum

½ egg white
2 ounces Genever Gin
2 ounces water
1½ ounce Jamaican Rum
1½ ounce Chartreuse
1½ ounce Gomme Syrup
½ ounce Orange Curaçao
½ ounce Angostura Bitters

Shake long and hard in an iced cocktail shaker, and strain into several chilled glasses.

When the Club took a leadership role in the fight to repeal the Eighteenth Amendment, it meant turning against the Republican Party. Guthrie (who had argued against the federal income tax in court) and Root led a legal attack on Prohibition that went all the way to the United States Supreme Court. When it became known that their client was a brewery, a humorist came up with a joke inspired by the name of a popular soft drink, Hires Root Beer: "Beer hires Root." [157] The Supreme Court affirmed the amendment in 1920.

Union League Club members were stirred up when a U.S. Senator (and Club member) who publicly opposed Prohibition, James W. Wadsworth, was defeated for reelection in 1926. The Club was the site of regular gatherings of "wets," some of them members, others visiting politicians and scholars like E.R. Seligman, a Columbia University economist. A nephew of former Union League Club Vice President Jesse Seligman, he presented an economic argument against Prohibition that had special appeal for businessmen: if the Eighteenth Amendment were repealed, the gain in tax revenue on alcohol would go far toward trimming the federal income tax. Although this and other anti-Prohibition lectures at the Club were described as private events, they stirred up complaints that the Union League was violating its founding principle of "absolute and unqualified loyalty" to the federal government.

Outside the Club, Root and his colleagues made a special effort to enlist the support of lawyers because they were in a position to challenge a law with which most of them disagreed. In a poll by the American Bar Association, 70 percent of the 20,000 members favored repeal of the Eighteenth Amendment. The Voluntary Committee of Lawyers, headed by Joseph H. Choate, Jr., lobbied the states and Congress to press forward with repeal by offering a new constitutional amendment. In February 1930, the Committee on Public Affairs (the new name for the Committee on Political Reform) distributed a questionnaire to Union League Club members, asking them to choose between three options: either Prohibition should be enforced more rigidly; the law should be amended to permit beer and wine; or the Eighteenth Amendment should be repealed. The Club then had 1,800 members. Of the 1,400 who replied, 8 percent demanded rigid enforcement, 20 percent wanted the law amended, and repeal was supported by 72 percent. [158]

When the Club reported the results of the poll to the newspapers, there were cries of disbelief that this important Republican institution cared so much about this one cause that it would oppose the Party. An editorial writer at the *Times* said he was certain that the Union League Club would support a Republican candidate for President, whether he was a "dry" or a "wet."[159] When it became known in 1930 that the new clubhouse under construction on Murray Hill contained a bar—a "sumptuous" one, according to one report—commentators speculated that the House Committee knew something that nobody else did. "Bar in New Union League Clubhouse Ready for Repeal of Prohibition Law," ran a headline.[160] This controversy must have bothered the Club officers because a photo spread of the new clubhouse that appeared in the Republican *Herald-Tribune* early in 1931 included not one photograph of the bar.[161]

In 1932, even as a new constitutional amendment ending Prohibition was being considered by Congress and state legislatures, the Club loyally organized a rally for the "bone dry" President Hoover at Madison Square Garden. Nonetheless, Root told friends that as much as he admired Hoover, he was certain that the President's support of Prohibition would come back to haunt him.

"He will be bitten by the very people he has tried to help," Root predicted, adding, "I think the Republican Party needs a licking."[162]

The man who imposed that licking was not a Union League Club member, but he did carry two important names in Club history. After Franklin Delano Roosevelt was elected President in 1932, Club President Charles C. Paulding tactfully invited him, "as Governor of New York and an eminent citizen," to the Club to be honored by a reception before he was inaugurated President. Equally tactfully, the President-elect replied that, as much as he would enjoy visiting the Club and greeting his friends there,

he was heading off on vacation, and "there will be practically no time left on my return."[163] So many Union League Club members voted for him (many even switching their party membership) that the Club reiterated the policy that adherence to Republican principles would be sufficient qualification for membership, with the final say to rest with the Committee on Admissions.

After Elihu Root died in 1937, in his sixtieth year of membership, the Club's memorial to him emphasized his devotion to the Club and his fellow members. The memorial quoted a letter he had sent to another senior member: "I congratulate you on being able to spend so much time in this interesting world, and upon having seen so much and having done so much. There is something very pleasing about the contemplation of old age, full of honor, with the battles all fought and rest well earned, and with the esteem and affection of a host of friends."[164]

The Union League Club, 1863–2013

152

The Park Avenue Clubhouse

"From the Atlantic to the Pacific I was entertained in many of the beautiful clubs," a well-known English travel writer, John Fraser, told a Club officer in the 1920s, "but the one that has left the most favorable impression upon me is your old Union League Club in New York."[166] "Old" was the governing word. As much as the members and their guests loved the charming third Clubhouse, its many years of heavy use had left it a little shabby and with a reputation as a fire trap. Its setting was changing even more rapidly. Once a quiet, distinguished uptown corner, Fifth Avenue and Thirty-Ninth Street had become a midtown shopping center. Every time the lease on the ground under the building was renegotiated, the rent went up.

Opposite: *The Union League Club Clubhouse, Park Avenue and Thirty-Seventh Street* (Vernon Howe Bailey 1934)

The officers were talking about moving as early as 1905, when they established a fund for a new building. Nothing came of it until after the war, when President James R. Sheffield, Henry Davison's successor, requested a $250,000 appropriation to rehabilitate the old building. Younger members objected that what the Club needed was not a patched-up old clubhouse, but a new one that addressed their interests. The new-building group, nicknamed "The Kickers," was initially outnumbered by the "Stickers," but they made converts. Sheffield withdrew his request and ordered a survey of the membership on their wants and needs. This survey revealed that, while the average age of membership was higher than ever, the younger members who represented the Club's future were living their lives in strikingly new ways that affected their use of the Club.

Historically, most business had been in the evening for drinks, billiards, or dinner. On Saturday or Sunday, members customarily walked over to the Club from their East Side townhouses or apartments for breakfast and a weekly haircut, stayed for lunch with friends, and whiled away the afternoon at the card or billiard tables.

This lifestyle was unavailable to the family men living in New Jersey, Westchester, or Long Island. With many members in the 1920s commuting to their jobs in the city from the suburbs, Club-going habits were changing. Their interest lay in weekday lunches with friends or for business purposes, a quick game of squash or pool, or a drink at the bar, before taking a commuter train or ferry home. Some nights, they would require a bed after the theater or a late meeting. These men of the new generation were saying that their wives would like to use the clubhouse more frequently and independently than an annual, carefully chaperoned visit on Ladies' Day.

The findings of the survey made new converts to the ranks of the Kickers. The Nominating Committee proposed that the next President be Alfred E. Marling, prominent in real estate and who was already negotiating for a building site right at the top of Murray Hill at Thirty-Seventh Street and Park Avenue.

Mary Murray's Lengthy Tea

One of the most distinctive residential areas in midtown Manhattan, Murray Hill was named for the Murray family who lived there for many years. It and they had roles in a famous patriotic story. After George Washington's forces lost the Battle of Brooklyn in 1776 and then escaped by crossing the East River to Manhattan, Mrs. Mary Murray was said to have distracted British officers from their pursuit by serving them a lengthy tea in her house on the hill. The Union League Club later honored Mrs. Murray when it renamed its former Ladies Dining Room for her, and hung a painting said to be of the scene by Emanuel Leutze in the Mary Murray Room.

Herbert L. Satterlee (Club President 1938-39)
(Left: Albert A. Rose; Right: Frank Hall Salisbury)
Satterlee and his Morgan in-laws helped the Club to acquire a plot on Murray Hill for the new Clubhouse.

The Murray Hill site was available to the Club because two brothers-in-law wanted to protect their residences from commercial development. One of these men was Herbert Livingston Satterlee, a New York lawyer, Assistant Secretary of the Navy during Theodore Roosevelt's second term as President, and a long-time Union League Club member and Club President 1938 to 1939. The other was his brother-in-law, J.P. "Jack" Morgan, Jr., the heir of J. Pierpont Morgan, who had died in 1913.

The father had been a Union League Club member for most of his life, but the son, who was a Democrat, did not join the Club until 1940, when Satterlee was Club President. The Morgans and Satterlee had large brownstone houses on the block at the top of Murray Hill. Satterlee's house was at the corner of Park and Thirty-Sixth, where apartment towers now stand. Mr. Morgan Sr.'s house on Madison at Thirty-Sixth had been owned by the Phelps Stokes family, who were related by marriage to the family of Club founder Robert Minturn. This building and his son's nearby big brownstone, at Thirty-Seventh and Madison, are now part of the Morgan Library & Museum.

The Morgan family worried that the land on the block they did

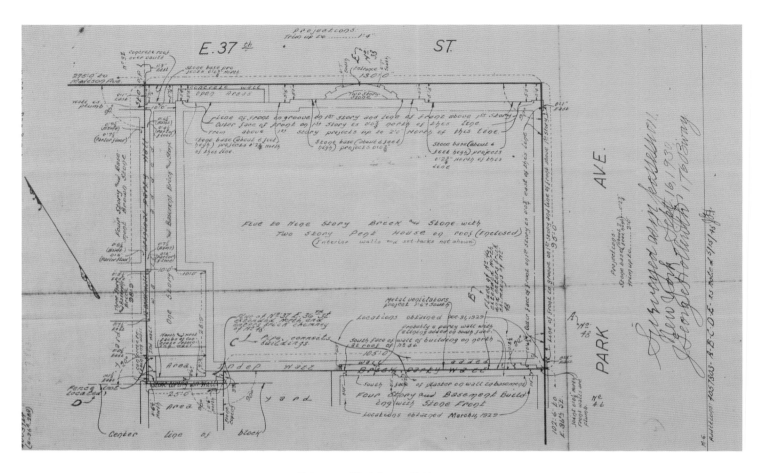

Plat survey of Park Avenue Clubhouse

not control would be taken over by developers who were transforming the Murray Hill area into a shopping district. When the courts refused to enforce nineteenth-century covenants that required only residential buildings on Murray Hill, the Morgans' real estate company acquired several more lots on the block, including a 90-foot by 130-foot parcel with several brownstone houses at the southwest corner, at Park and Thirty-Seventh. The new owners let it be known that this property might be made available to the right buyer whose plans met the family's standards. The building must be a traditional granite, brick, and limestone structure that did not dominate the block, squeeze neighboring buildings, or cast a shadow over the Satterlee house and the Morgans' gardens. If the buyer agreed to those conditions, the parcel was offered at $200,000, the Morgans' purchase price.

This offer very definitely interested the Union League Club. President Marling presented the plan to the membership in mailings and at a meeting that, by every account, was lengthy and emotional. Even members who believed the sale of the old building was necessary felt torn, so strong were their ties to the Fifth Avenue building in which the Club had lived and thrived for

Alfred E. Marling (President 1928-30)
(Ernest Ipsen, 1932)

THE UNION LEAGUE CLUB
DINNER
IN HONOR OF
EX-PRESIDENT ALFRED E. MARLING
AND
PRESIDENT CHARLES COOK PAULDING

The members celebrated the successful move to the new clubhouse
in the traditional way with a dinner in honor of two of their Presidents.

almost half a century. "I think most of us wanted to stay here if we could," said one member, "but the logic of the situation inexorably led us finally to the conclusions as stated in that report." When worry was voiced about the cost of a new building, a member recalled that, a year earlier when the members were asked to donate funds for Herbert Hoover's 1928 presidential campaign, "it came out so easy that some of the people on the campaign committee were sorry they had not asked for two campaigns at once." Another member thought there was but one choice: "In fact it seems to me, Mr. President, that the whole thing can be put in a nutshell: the question is shall the Union League Club stand still or shall it take a step forward?" As applause and cheers broke out in the room, he went on: "In this big City of New York, which is bound to be the greatest city in the world, if it is not today, and in this Union League Club with its traditions, its magnificent traditions, I say we cannot afford to stand still. If we stand still we take a step backward."

The vote was 307 to 90 in favor of moving, but nobody was elated. Recalled a member, "We left the hall that night in the mood of men filing out from a funeral."[167]

The challenge was to build a new clubhouse that met the Morgans' expectations, met modern-day requirements, and still retained the old building's charm and beauty. Satisfying these expectations was the duty of the Chairman of the Building Committee, Charles C. Paulding, a nephew of former Club President Chauncey Depew. Everybody was in agreement about the architect, Benjamin Wistar Morris III. Born in Oregon, the son of an Episcopal bishop, he was related to the Morgans by marriage, and had joined the Union League Club in 1922. Trained at Columbia and the École de Beaux Arts in Paris, Morris specialized in large public buildings with a classical appearance. He had designed or co-designed the New York Public Library at Bryant Park, the annex to the Morgan Library, the Cunard Building at the Battery, and a new Metropolitan Opera House (which was not built). When the Cunard Line built the *Queen Mary* in the 1930s, Morris was retained to design staterooms. He was known for his sensitivity to his clients' needs and aims. Morris, said the head of the Metropolitan Opera Guild, Otto Kahn, "has a very accurate conception of the public he is dealing with and of certain basic and insurmountable factors in the situation."[168]

The Union League Club wanted something grand and classical, and also familiar and comfortable. The Club got all four in an eleven-story building that cost the Club a little under $3,500,000. An architectural study of the building summarizes the style this way: "In spite of the current popularity of the Art Deco style in New York City, the Union League was designed in a historical style. Faced with red brick and limestone, the elevations deliberately recall the architecture of eighteenth-century England and the American colonies, often called the Georgian style."[169]

This understated style has been used in the design of other clubs, as well as in residences and official buildings. The Union League Clubhouse has two different appearances, depending on the viewer's point of view. On the Park Avenue side, the building is imposing, but around the corner on tree-lined Thirty-Seventh Street, the structure seems much more intimate. Inside, borrowing a look from the old clubhouse, Morris produced a double stairway with curved balustrades grandly swinging up from the foyer. "Climbing the central staircase from the ground floor into the main foyer, one feels interior space expanding into a grand statement," a visitor has observed. "This effect relies on the double-height ceiling (which appears triple-height from the front door), the great carved lintels leading into the Main Lounge and Billiards Room, and the open bay over the staircase with a window on the Club Room."[170]

Other parts of the new clubhouse that also seem inspired by the Fifth Avenue building include the expansive Members Lounge running the length of the Park Avenue side, with a broad view of the street from nearby chairs; the Cabinet Room floor dedicated to a suite of private dining and meeting rooms; and the large Library with its quiet, comfortable corners and adjoining rows of bookcases. Among the new features was a hotel facility with more than sixty guest rooms for the increasing population of members who lived out of town or in the suburbs and needed a home away from home.

Another innovation was an athletic facility, with a small gymnasium, a Turkish bath, and squash courts. For many members, squash was as important to Club membership as billiards and, before that, dominoes had long been for their seniors—not just a challenging game, but an opportunity to meet other members and become part of Club life.

The new feature that attracted the most comment was the facility for women guests in a dedicated Ladies Dining Room and Lounge, accessible through a special Ladies Entrance on Park Avenue and express elevator to the fourth floor. Women had played significant roles in the Club's history. Wives, daughters, and mothers of the founders had organized the Sanitary Commission Fairs

Charles Cook Paulding (President 1931-1938)
(George Burroughs Torrey)

and presented the colors to the Twentieth Colored Regiment. The anniversary of the Club's founding often coincided with one of the Club's two Ladies Days. All the same, when the Nineteenth Amendment to the Constitution, extending the vote to women, was under consideration in New York State in 1914, a vote at a Club meeting was overwhelmingly in opposition. After the amendment passed in 1917, there was no reviewing stand outside the Clubhouse to greet the march of suffragettes, some of whom as they passed cheerfully shouted, "Tories!"[171]

A separate entrance and facility for women may seem archaic today, but in 1931, making any space for women in a club like the Union League Club bordered on revolutionary. After some protests by the old guard, the new Clubhouse had a formal Ladies Dining Room and an adjacent Lounge with knotted pine tables. The public was impressed. Of the six photographs chosen for the *New York Herald Tribune*'s coverage of the Clubhouse's opening in February 1931, two were of the Ladies Dining Room and Lounge.[172] A writer from *The New Yorker* toured the building. Like a witty youngster with an elderly uncle, the magazine and the Club had a teasing but fond relationship that was sometimes expressed in cartoons showing elderly gentlemen ensconced in overstuffed chairs. This time, however, *The New Yorker*'s representative was seriously impressed, especially with the Ladies' facility that the writer called "the Great Change."[173]

In his speech at the laying of the cornerstone for the new Clubhouse, former Club President James R. Sheffield (1921 to 1924) stressed continuity: "Into this cornerstone there goes more than documents—it safeguards our faith. We reverently place in its keeping the memorials of a past glorified by service and the hopes of a future made better and more secure by the influence of the traditions of our founders and their successor membership in the Union League Club." Among the documents placed in the cornerstone was a letter from former Club President Charles Evans Hughes, Chief Justice of the Supreme Court. He expressed the wish that "the benediction of the past will rest graciously on the new venture," and predicted, "The new home will be irradiated

Saying Good Bye

At the final members meeting at the Fifth Avenue Clubhouse, in December 1930, President Marling remarked on "the comfortable, happy, and, on occasion, uproarious times we have had here," "the wonderful patriotic and political processions we have watched," "our quiet and dignified Library," and, of course, the building's role in history: "Presidents of the United States have spoken from the rostrum, and members of Cabinets, Senators, Congressmen, and Governors have been our guests within the four walls of this hall."[174]

In January 1932, the old Clubhouse was mostly destroyed by a fire. As the blaze burned through a cold January night, the hundreds of spectators who looked included a group described by a reporter as "a handful of elderly gentlemen who are members of the Club." Among the losses were the stained-glass windows designed by John La Farge and Louis Comfort Tiffany that had been left behind when the Club moved out. [175]

with the same spirit and I have no doubt that the patriotic fervor which brought the Club into being will give zest to its renewed endeavors."[176] To persuade hesitant members that this could be the case in the new building, President Charles Paulding wrote a pamphlet, titled *Do You Know Your Club?* that served as a guide to all the new rooms, hallways, and corners of the premises. It ended with the words, "It is *your* Club."[177]

The old members needed no instructions. As the furniture arrived in the new building, one elderly man was seen pushing a chair across the lounge from the spot where the movers had left it. "This is my regular chair," he explained, "and it belongs at the southerly window of the Park Avenue side."[178]

Carrying on the Old Order

The First World War and, later, the Great Depression were so enveloping that it comes as something of a shock to realize that, outside of some economizing, the Club's daily life changed very little during those years. Breakfast, lunch, and dinner were served seven days a week. A barber provided shaves and haircuts from 7:30 a.m. to 7 p.m. on weekdays and Saturday, and sometimes on Sunday morning. The Committee on Art organized a new exhibition every month. (The final exhibition in the Fifth Avenue Clubhouse was "Portraits of Eminent Jurists and Other Notables.") The Committee on Public Affairs, formerly the Committee on Political Reform, debated political and social issues. The *Yearbook* (known as the "blue book" because that was the usual color of its binding) kept up the traditions of honoring the Club's role in creating the Civil War Colored Regiments and listing the names of every member who had been born in the nineteenth century.

Opposite: Union League Club Presidents, 1863-1903 (Otto Stark)

This is a typical big, enthusiastic turnout for the children's Christmas Party, which was put on by member Lloyd Taylor.

The central event for many members remained the monthly meetings. Its customs remained unchanged from the 1870s. Special events were a little more improvised, with appearances by Republican presidential candidates, businessmen, economists, an expert in modern technology and the occasional controversial figure, such as a labor union leader. A New York police captain once came in and described the miracles of modern radio, at least as far as it concerned law enforcement. A committee might put on a movie night featuring travel to an exotic land. Father-and-Son Days were especially popular at a club in which membership was a tradition in many families. The Club or the committees occasionally gave a luncheon or dinner honoring members who were war veterans or noted humanitarians. One of the favorite charitable events was the Christmas Entertainment for Crippled Children, organized for many years by member Lloyd Taylor for 200 or more boys who were brought to the Clubhouse from a special needs hospital to meet Santa and other special guests (Lou Gehrig appeared one year).

When neighborhood children crashed the party, Taylor tolerantly announced, "Well, it's Christmas," and allowed them to stay and accept a present.[179]

Some members regarded the Billiard Room as the heart of the Club, and it was treated that way. In the 1880s, a member named Charles A. Fowler cared enough about it to donate two stained glass windows designed by John La Farge, each with a centerpiece containing the Club's monogram. These windows remained in the old Clubhouse and were destroyed by the fire after the Club moved out.

Passion for billiards was not universal. The Billiard Room Attendant for forty years, John H. McCrea, told a reporter that he had seen only one banker at the tables, and that, "though he has seen many Presidents, he never saw one of them handling a cue."[183] Proud as pool players were, this was a spectator-friendly sport. In one long-remembered performance, an eight-year-old boy wonder, Willie Hoppe, was brought to the Club in 1895 to demonstrate his skills. His manager, Maurice Day, dressed him in a small tuxedo, explaining (as Hoppe recalled in his memoirs), "These Union League folks are tony and you've got to dress up a bit for them." Hoppe was impressed by the Club's facilities. "This was vastly different from the billiard room in Brooklyn or any other billiard room I had played in. There were oil paintings on the wall and thick rugs on the floor." His demonstration must have been sensational because several members presented him with $50, a small fortune for a boy at that time.[184]

The City's leading amateur player was Wilson P. Foss, of whom it was said by a billiards writer, "He could have made himself the professional champion of the world."[185] After winning several national championships without losing a game, Foss joined the Union League Club, and became the Billiard Room's guiding spirit—coaching, encouraging, and organizing players and the spring and fall championships. He arranged for professional coaches, one of whom was Erich Hagenlacher, a former sergeant in the German army who had won a Balkline world championship as well as a biathlon consisting solely of competition in chess and pool. Hagenlacher coached and taught at the Club for many years before returning to Germany in 1938.

Other types of games arrived at the Club as a vision of physical fitness swept through America in the early twentieth century. At the same time Theodore Roosevelt was propounding the doctrine of "the strenuous life," psychologists were advising workaholic Americans to "dodge the deadly habit of industry" and shed the bulk that, in the Gilded Age, had been considered a sign of

Captain Miles and the Card Players

The staff was regularly praised. "We have reason to be proud of our staff of loyal, competent, and trustworthy employees," said the Club's Executive Committee in 1939. "Their devotion to the interests of the Club and to the accommodation of its individual members is exceptional in spirit and accomplishment." [180] In the new Clubhouse, dominoes and card players—the latter playing the new evolution of whist called contract bridge—settled into the Card Room Café. Some members played cards all day Saturday, went home and dressed for dinner, and returned for more play until the room's Captain, W. Seldon Miles, produced his famous late supper of Welsh rarebit.

A former slave, Captain Miles arrived at the Fifth Avenue Clubhouse at the age of twenty in 1881, working alongside former Pullman porters and veterans of the Colored Regiments to keep members supplied with food and drink. Sometimes he played Santa at the Crippled Children's Party. In 1941, he was awarded his twelfth gold stripe to put on his jacket, one each for every five years at the Union League Club. He told the newspaper reporters invited for the occasion that he had served every Republican President from Benjamin Harrison to Herbert Hoover. Theodore Roosevelt would cry out, "Miles, you old rascal! Are you still here?" The headline over the *Times* story read, "No Democrat, He."[181]

Another longtime staff member, Joseph Queenan, started out as a score marker in the Billiard Room and rose to head waiter in the Main Dining Room. According to the report of his retirement in 1938 in an African-American newspaper, he was a member of several fraternal associations, including the Clubmen's Beneficial League and the Union League Social and Benevolent Club.[182]

manly success.[186] "*Keep in Trim*—that is Wall Street's imperative axiom," noted a journalist. "Not only is it necessary for the 'climbers' in Wall Street to watch their physical condition for the Money Battle, but it is also a matter of moment to the biggest men, the greatest financial figures."

Besides sponsoring bowling teams that used the alley that the Club belatedly installed in the Fifth Avenue Clubhouse, the Club had golf and tennis teams that played on weekends at the country clubs that sprang up in the suburbs in the early twentieth century. This athletic spirit developed further with the introduction of squash when courts opened in the new Clubhouse in 1931.

The Club's rarest competition was the race to be the most senior member. The game was played with good humor. In 1936, the number five man on the list, eighty-nine-year-old George B. Mathews, assured them, "I shall strive with all my brawn and sinew to reach first place." He asked the Club Secretary to send him the names and addresses of other senior members. "I may wish to write to them, just for the fun of it, and send them a boyish challenge to prove what stock they're made of." President Paulding was so charmed that he wrote back with the information. Elihu Root was number one on the list and Erickson Perkins was number two, followed by Edward Van Volkenburgh and John D. Rockefeller. When Mr. Mathews finally reached the top of the list in 1941, his wife reported that he fully intended to continue on as always, relying on "the routine of living which, after sixty years, has carried him to the top."[187]

The enthusiasm for fitness tended to discourage the elaborate seven-course meals that used to be served in the Gilded Age. Still, members did have food preferences that sometimes evolved into Club traditions. The Club kitchen was also known for its green turtle soup, its Christmas mince pies, and its Virginia-cured hams made up especially for the Union League Club.[188] When William E. Barker, a fervent New Englander, joined the Club, he was so dismayed by what the menu called "chowder" that he complained to the House Committee. In a restaurant that, in the 1940s, served 600 meals a day (and brought in $500,000 a year),

few priorities were higher than keeping members happy with their food. The chef started all over again with his chowder, and before long, Wednesday at the members' table was designated fish chowder day. Members who ordered it toasted the name of Mr. Barker.

Depression and War

The Finance Committee, headed by former Club Treasurer George E. Baker, invested in the stock market successfully until it fortuitously liquidated its investments in July 1929. The Depression soon took its toll on the Club. In 1931, there were 1,818 dues-paying members and the deficit was just under $4,000. Despite a reduction in the initiation fee to $100 from $300, the membership fell to 1,480 in 1935 and 1,308 in 1939, with the deficit sometimes running over $30,000. Austerity measures included ending the traditional monthly members meeting in 1937. House Committee Chairman and, later, Club President Alfred H. Cosden devoted himself to the Club full-time, living in the Clubhouse and visiting or corresponding with other clubs and hotels around the country.

By 1945, the mortgage on the building was cut nearly in half. In gratitude, the Club elected Cosden as its first Life Member. When he stepped down as President, Cosden celebrated the Club's historic mission, not his own improvements: "This old patriotic organization of ours, founded in 1863 to support good government, should be a leader in such undertakings. To be a place only to eat, meet a friend, and play a game is not enough. The interest that we, as a Club, take in problems that are for the common good of all people will be the measure of our success."[189]

One problem was the fear of a war that many members of the Club were sure was coming. When the respected journalist Dorothy Thompson was invited in 1938 to be the first woman to address the Club, the title she chose for her speech, "A Nation of Speculators," might have led businessmen to believe that they would be criticized. What the capacity audience heard, however, was a classic Union League Club address on public ethics and the need for public responsibility and action. As she reported on what

Alfred H. Cosden (President 1940-45)
(Paul Trebilcock)

A New Club Symbol

Perhaps it was the prospect of the second major war within a generation that stimulated member Henry L. Stoddard to decide that the Club's symbol should be changed. A newspaper editor, historian, and political writer, Stoddard became interested in this issue when he wrote a brief history of the Club for its seventy-fifth anniversary in 1938. Later, in his eighties, he served as the Club's Secretary from 1939 to 1942 and founded the Club *Bulletin*.

Stoddard was not fond of the Club's heraldic image of the griffin, the defender of valuable objects that is seen on many warriors' shields. Preferring a patriotic symbol borrowed from nature, not mythology, he commissioned some sketches from Tiffany's and selected the American bald eagle without the arrows of war in its talons and looking to the viewer's right, which generally denotes peace. After two years of discussion and debate, it appeared on the Club's stationery and china.

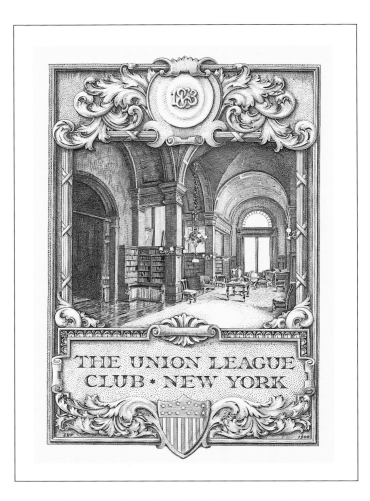

The Club's bookplate is the work of Edwin Davis French, America's foremost engraver.

she had recently seen and experienced in Germany, she made it clear that the Nazis were a threat to civilization. On her return home, she was also appalled that the American obsession with material well-being blocked moral concern and dedicated action in response to the totalitarian threat. "We admire success and are callous to achievement."[190] When members began to volunteer for military service in 1940, the Club initiated a series of talks on the subject of "True Americanism."

World War II was a new type of great conflict, managed by professionals with little room for the likes of volunteer colonels like Theodore Roosevelt and William Hayward. One of the Club's few career soldiers was Ulysses S. Grant, III. A grandson of the Civil War General and President, he was a West Point graduate in the class of 1903 and an engineer. In World War II, Major General Grant commanded the country's Civil Defense operations. Another 157 members served in uniform in the European

Mr. Child's Library

Of the 165 employees in 1940, seventeen had twenty or more years of service. Among the most senior men were two Captains, W. Seldon Miles (sixty years) and John H. McCrea (forty-six years), and the Club Librarian, William Bradford Child (forty-five years). Formerly a librarian in a divinity school, Mr. Child was comfortably at home in the Club's distinguished collection of leather-bound limited editions and classic texts. In a library where new or popular books tended to be looked down on (a Library Committee Chairman put them in the category of "current and more or less ephemeral literature"), anybody looking for *Gone with the Wind* was likely to be directed to one of the lending libraries in the neighborhood. In other ways, Mr. Child worked at the cutting edge of his profession, introducing adjustable shelving so books could be arranged by topic and not size, and creating the Club's first card catalog. In his long tenure, the Union League Club's book collection nearly doubled from 9,000. A visiting *Times* reporter described Mr. Child as "a quiet, bald, scholarly man who takes pride in the beautiful 17,000-volume library over which he presides." [191]

Among the regulars in the Library in the 1930s and 1940s was a retired publisher and editor named S. S. McClure. Half a century earlier, his name was in the title of one of the country's most popular periodicals, *McClure's Magazine*, which introduced many Americans to the works of Rudyard Kipling, Sir Arthur Conan Doyle, Robert Lewis Stevenson, Willa Cather, and the Swiss educational reformer Maria Montessori. *McClure's* also published a number of well-known social critics, including Ida Tarbell and Lincoln Steffens, whose exposés were so critical that Theodore Roosevelt chastised them as "muckrakers." Forced to sell his magazines and book publishing operation, McClure disappeared from public life, but he found a home in the Union League Club Library where, surrounded by his personal papers, he labored over his memoirs, which he never did complete.

This was the world of Mr. Child in his elegant outpost at the Union League. After interviewing him and other senior staff members, the *Times* reporter concluded his article on an understanding note: "In the light of these unusual service records, it would seem that the old order, in the midst of a changing world, has a habit of 'carrying on' at the Union League Club." [192]

or Pacific theaters. The first of the Club's more than 100 casualties in the war was Hallsted L. Hopping, a Navy pilot shot down during a raid on the Gilbert Islands in February 1942 and the first aircraft squadron commander to lose his life in the war. A destroyer escort was named in his honor.

Many members served the country out of uniform. Harvey Gibson, who had assisted Henry Davison in 1918, headed the American Red Cross Commission to Great Britain and Western Europe. This was the third war—after the Civil War and World War I—in which one of the most important and effective medical services was under the oversight of a Union League Club member. At home, the Club sold war bonds, rationed its food and liquor, set aside 4,800 pounds of scrap metal, loaned office space to the Murray Hill air wardens, and provided volunteers for the City Patrol Committee, a volunteer anti-sabotage operation.

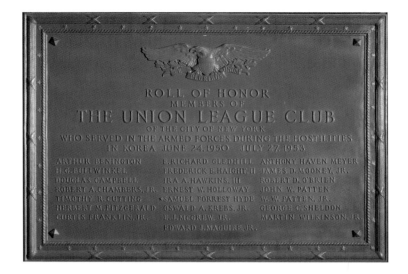

Plaque listing Club members who served in the hostilities in Korea.

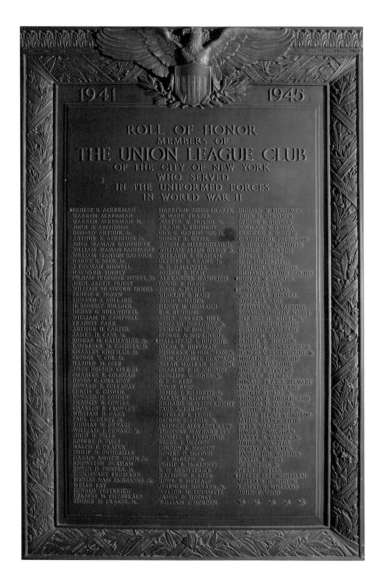

Plaque recognizing the service of Club members who served in World War II.

Honorary Members 1927–1964

Honorary Member	Elected to Honorary Membership	Admitted to Regular Membership (if applicable)	Notable Achievements
Henry Thomas Mayo	May 12, 1927		Rear Admiral, United States Navy
Albert Gleaves	May 12, 1927		Vice Admiral, United States Navy
William Wallace Atterbury	May 12, 1927		Brigadier General, United States Army
Enoch H. Crowder	May 29, 1927		Major General, United States Army
George F. Baker	1928	1868	Treasurer, Union League Club, Philanthropist and President of First National Bank (forerunner of Citibank)
Herbert Hoover	1929		President of the United States
Charles Curtis	April 11, 1929		Vice President of the United States
Charles H. Thomas	1934	1877	
Erickson Perkins	1934	1878	
George B. Matthews	1936	1880	
Charles P. Fagnani	1937	1902	Professor, Union Theological Seminary
Charles L. Tappin	1938	1887	
Henry L. Stoddard	1943	1900	Journalist who covered and interviewed President Ulysses S. Grant during his final illness. Owner of the New York newspaper *The Evening Mail*. Secretary, Union League Club
Henry L. Stimson	1946		United States Secretary of War, United States Secretary of State, and Governor-General of the Philippines
George C. Marshall	1946		General of the Army, United States Secretary of Defense, and United States Secretary of State
Ernest J. King	1946		Fleet Admiral, United States Navy
Dwight D. Eisenhower	1946		General of the Army, United States Army and Chief of Staff of the United States Army when made an honorary member. President of the United States
Douglas MacArthur	1946		General of the Army, United States Army
Henry H. Arnold	1946		General of the Army, United States Army and General of the Air Force, United States Air Force
Chester W. Nimitz	1946		Fleet Admiral, United States Navy
Alexander A. Vandegrift	1946		Medal of Honor Recipient and General and Commandant of the United States Marine Corps
Dudley Phelps	1947	1886	
James V. Forrestal	1949		United States Secretary of Defense
Richard M. Nixon	1953 and 1988		President of the United States
Edward Ridley Finch	1953	1909	Justice, New York Supreme Court and New York State Assemblyman
Withers A. Burress	1953		Lieutenant General, United States Army
Arthur D. Struble	1954		Admiral, United States Navy
Leon W. Johnson	1954		Medal of Honor Recipient and General, United States Air Force
Thomas W. Herren	1955		Lieutenant General, United States Army
Charles B. Stone III	1956		Lieutenant General, United States Air Force
Frederick W. McMahon	1956		Vice Admiral, United States Navy
William E. Hall	1957		Medal of Honor Recipient and Lieutenant Commander of the United States Naval Reserve
Blackshear M. Bryan	1958		Lieutenant General, United States Army
Thomas S. Combs	1960		Vice Admiral, United States Navy, Commandant, Third Naval District
Charles Wellburn, Jr.	1960		
Edward J. O'Neill	1961		Lieutenant General, United States Army
Henry C. Hodges, Jr.	1961	1932	Major General, United States Army
Garrison H. Davidson	1962		Lieutenant General, United States Army
Harold T. Deutermann	1963		Vice Admiral, United States Navy
Robert W. Porter, Jr.	1964		General, United States Army

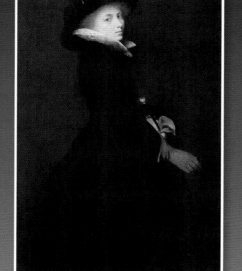

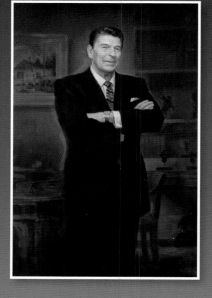

IKE
The Board of Governors authorizes a portrait of Honorary Member, President Dwight D. Eisenhower to be painted and displayed in the Clubhouse alongside portraits of other Republican Presidents.

100 YEARS
The Club celebrates its centennial anniversary with a recording by the Union League Club Chorus and publications honoring its long history of contribution to the nation. Member Ulysses S. Grant III chairs the Civil War Centennial Commission.

WOMEN MEMBERS
The Club first accepts women members and quickly accommodates itself to the new order. The Ladies Lounge is renamed the Mary Murray Room.

PRESIDENT REAGAN AT THE CLUB
He accepts Honorary Membership. Later, his portrait is presented to the Club, and alumni of his administration gather to celebrate his memory.

1956

1963

1989

1990

Part Four

The Modern Era

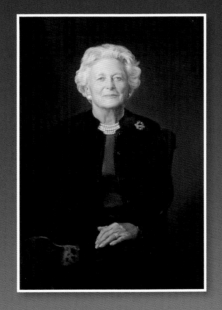

THE BOND WITH THE MILITARY
"I feel humble and privileged when sitting under the portraits of Grant, Sherman, and Sheridan in the Grant Room," says a member. A majority of Honorary Members are military officers. The Club hosts forty disabled soldiers and their guests for the Hope and Possibility Road Race in Central Park.

VISITS BY PRESIDENTS BUSH
George H. W. Bush visits frequently. President and Mrs. Bush's portraits are displayed in the Club. George W. Bush unveils his portrait and (like his father) receives the Theodore Roosevelt American Experience Award.

CELEBRATING THE HERITAGE
The Club reconnects with its past when it celebrates the centennial of the Statue of Liberty.

1997

2012

2012

The Club at 100

The spirit of carrying on, with one foot in the past and one in the present, was kept alive for decades in a series of engaging stories about a New York resident whom the world knew as "Father." Written in the 1930s by a man named Clarence Day and published in *The New Yorker*, these accounts were collected in a best-selling book, *Life with Father*, that in turn led to a play of that name that ran for 3,224 performances (it is still the longest running non-musical play in Broadway history), then to a hit movie with the same title that starred William Powell, Irene Dunn, and Elizabeth Taylor, and finally to a television series during the 1950s.

Opposite: Commemorative Cards
for Club and Members' Anniversaries

The subject was a family of New Yorkers "of the best sort" headed by a slightly eccentric, quite opinionated, and at heart very good man whose life was lived in three well-protected, inviolate rooms: his home, his office, and his club. "Father was a sociable man," wrote Day; "he liked to sit and talk with us at home, and with his friends at the Club."[193] Father's attempts to instill this strict sense of order into his rambunctious red-headed boys were often futile, but always entertaining to the millions of Americans unsettled by the great disorders of the Depression, World War II, and their aftermath.

Life with Father often seemed too good to be true, yet it was not fiction but a personal memoir (though undoubtedly the facts were embellished from time to time). "Father," also named Clarence Day, was a real man and also a member of the Union League Club for many years. He served in the Civil War in the New York Seventh Regiment, lived in the City all his life, worked successfully in Wall Street, knew and socialized with members of the City's old families, played billiards for long stretches, smoked Havana cigars, was fiercely opinionated on the subject of politics (a line in the movie version of *Life with Father* goes, "I don't know why God created damned fools and Democrats"), and was sufficiently respected at the Club to be appointed to the important Nominating and Executive committees.

From what his son wrote, we also know that, like many members, he used the Club as an oasis where he could escape to shake off the dust and debris of the trials of daily life. Whenever there were problems at home—say, when a new maid or cook did not meet his exacting standards, or one of his sons plugged the postman with a snowball and required a stern lecture—Father escaped to his Club, where great matters were either forgotten or decided. His son recalled the first thing Father did when he discovered he was gaining weight:

"What the saloon was to poor men and what coffeehouses had once been to Londoners, his club was to Father. It was the front and center of his social life. He stopped there for half an hour or so on his way home from the office, or he walked down there at nine in the evening when Mother had gone up to bed. He played a game or two of billiards—not cards—or he had a whisky and soda with Commodore Brown, or he met and sized up distinguished foreigners, whom he usually didn't think much of. Or he sought for advice about fat. Some members recommended long walks, but Father had always done a good deal of walking. The opinion of the Club was that in that case he had better take up riding horseback.

Which, of course, Father promptly did, acquiring a horse and joining a riding club."[194]

The Union League Club was so important to him that, after his death and that of his son and biographer in 1935, the Day family arranged for the Yale University Press to donate copies of books it published to the Club's library in Father's memory.

In some ways, the Union League Club before the 1950s was Father's fixed, hospitable, dependable oasis in an increasingly noisy and conflicted world. Any changes were small. For example, the Club continued its long tradition of sponsoring regular art exhibitions in the small hall just off the entrance lobby. While most of them included traditional or (from time to time) modern art by professional artists, there also was a new, popular, well-attended annual exhibition of members' special interests called "The Exhibition of Whims and Hobbies."[195]

One member presented his collection of objects related to the famous nineteenth-century singer Jenny Lind, "the Swedish Nightingale." Another displayed a large number of unusual canes carved from Puerto Rican magnolia. Other hobbies (or whims) included collections of fans, cartoons, wax portraits, orchids, even knives for paring apples. One of these hobbyists, reported a visiting journalist, had a look of "sheer joy . . . on his face" as he showed off his idiosyncratic collection.[196]

There were other obsessions. One was squash. The demand was such that the three squash courts in the new building were modernized with ventilating systems (and, later, air conditioning), a small laundry was set up, and the former barber shop was converted to a ping-pong room where the players could warm up for the increasingly serious matches in the popular inter-club

President Dwight D. Eisenhower
(Thomas Stephens, 1956)

Metropolitan League, where the Club's three teams were coached by the highly respected, long-time professional, John Collopy. The highlight of the season for the squash players—as for the tennis, billiards, and golf teams—remained the match with the Union League of Philadelphia.

Of course, politics remained another popular activity as the Club continued to honor the founders' mission of establishing "an association of men, under an organization of a social character, frankly exchanging views on great questions and disseminating them." Because debates over "great questions" were getting a little heated, the Public Affairs Committee evolved into the Committee on Special Activities for a few years. In 1950, the Public Affairs Committee was restored and began inviting public figures to speak at monthly Public Affairs Forums.

Where Will the Ladies Dine?

In 1945, with peace finally in hand, the Club was busier than it had been in years. It had 1,700 members, 460 more than in 1941 (almost half that gain was in 1944). Despite wartime restrictions, the Club did nearly $800,000 in business in 1944 and had a net operating profit of nearly $74,000. The four largest sources of income were the restaurant, then the bar, the hotel, and the cigar stand, which that year took in $34,000—the equivalent of $443,000 today. The building was so busy and crowded that President Howard C. Shepherd, in 1947, requested everyone to "be considerate in the use of the guest privilege" and make room for their fellow members at the dining tables and the bar.[197] Nine years later, in 1956, membership was 1,861 (the largest ever), the Club enjoyed a small profit, and the Campaign Committee raised $35,690 from 590 members to help President Eisenhower's reelection, and the Board of Governors authorized that a portrait of Eisenhower be painted by an artist of his choice.

When President LeRoy A. Peterson closed his report with these seemingly bland words, "A friendly Club spirit has continued to prevail, upon which, of course, the entire success of the Club depends," he might have had his fingers crossed because the next

item on the agenda was a matter that had already stimulated considerable unfriendly spirit: the Board proposed that women be admitted into the Main Dining Room.[198] This was an unanticipated consequence of one of the Park Avenue Clubhouse's most notable successes. When the Club established the Ladies Dining Room on the fourth floor (in the space that is now the Mary Murray Room), the other social areas in the Clubhouse were reserved for men except on Ladies Day and a few other special occasions. The rules were widely understood. Wives and other female relations of the Club members, as well as the widows of deceased Club members, were welcome at the Union League Club on a daily basis, so long as they stayed on the fourth floor. Club members were entitled to use the space only when accompanied by a woman who was qualified to be there. This was overseen by the Ladies Department of the Club staff, which reported to manager Edward P. Newton, a modest Englishman who arrived at the Club in 1936, retired in 1962, and was described by one grateful Club President as "efficient" and "dignified."[199]

The rules for family use in the rest of the Club were somewhat more intricate. A wife could enter the building at the main entrance when she was with her husband, but if they were apart, she was required to use the Park Avenue entrance. A Union League Club member was permitted to stay with his wife in a Club bedroom overnight, but not permitted to eat breakfast with her the next morning in the Main Dining Room. So many husbands, wives, and daughters ate together on the fourth floor that the Ladies Dining Room was nicknamed the Family Dining Room, and the Club had to turn away many women and their guests. In 1956, the House Committee decided that the only way to stop members' wives from going off to Schrafft's was to set aside tables for them in the Main Dining Room. While this made business sense, the officers knew enough to prepare the Club. The problem was described humorously as follows: "The code that ladies are never discussed at a men's club was breached many times as members discussed the seemingly insoluble problem of how to call on the ladies for support while preventing the ladies literally from calling on them."[200] The House Committee and Board of Governors sent two letters of explanation to every member, and arranged for a poll of the membership that came out resoundingly in favor of the idea of allowing wives in the Main Dining Room, 1,219 members in favor and 182 opposed.

When the officers took the issue to the annual meeting in February 1957, a great many members were eager to speak against the proposed new policy. A bylaw in the Club's constitution required that resolutions instructing a committee be posted on the Club bulletin board at least fifteen days before a members meeting. No such posting had been made, but President Peterson welcomed informal discussion at the end of the meeting. There was plenty of that, including a motion for a special meeting to resolve the issue. Although this resolution also was not countenanced by the bylaws, another member went ahead and seconded it, anyway, and (to quote the minutes) "commented at some length as to his objections to the House Committee's proposal." The discussion went on so long that President Peterson had to leave to catch a plane. When the chair *pro tem* allowed an informal, non-binding "expression of opinion," a majority of the remaining 100 members in the room voted in favor of having a special meeting to debate and decide "the matter of the use of the Main Dining Room by ladies."[201]

That was enough controversy to persuade the officers to cancel their plan. The House Committee promised to enlarge the Ladies Dining Room, sometime in the future.

Club History

In the 1940s, the Club commissioned a new history (the second after Henry W. Bellows' 1879 book) from a professional writer, Will Irwin, whose books included a biography of Herbert Hoover. After his death, the book was completed by Earl Chapin May and Joseph Hotchkiss. The result was a warm, affectionate, often humorous narrative of the Club's activities and convictions. A reviewer called the book "a contribution to American history and particularly to the history of the Republican Party, of which the Union League Club

A Founder's Diary

The year 1952 was a banner year for the Union League Club in the public eye. The Irwin club history was published that year, and so was the four-volume edition of the diary that Club founder George Templeton Strong kept between 1835 and 1875 (a fifth volume on the Civil War years was published a decade later). The lead editor of the *Diary*, the dean of American historians, Allen Nevins of Columbia University, described it in language usually reserved for historical novels: Strong presented "a sweeping panorama of social and political change." Often the centerpiece of that panorama was the Union League Club. No other source brings alive so well the tensions and fears of New Yorkers at the time of the Civil War. Few books reveal so much about the inner life of an idealistic but usually realistic man struggling to make a better world in demanding times—in other words a fairly typical Union League Club member of the best sort.

has been an inner citadel through its eighty-eight years," yet politics was only a part of the story told by Irwin and his co-authors.[202]

The Club's previous anniversaries had been marked with a dinner with many speeches and toasts, followed by admiring stories in the city's newspapers and, eventually, publication of the long night's proceedings as meticulously recorded by stenographers. The Public Affairs Committee, which organized the centennial, spread the celebration throughout the year with a variety of events. From the opening luncheon in February to an open house in December, the Club hosted special events, including a celebration of the anniversary of the first Ladies Night and Housewarming, exhibitions in the art gallery and the library, several history-related evenings and

Union League Centennial Proclamation

The centennial year opened with a formal proclamation that was posted in the lobby and outside Lincoln Hall.

One hundred years ago, in a time of grave national crisis, the Union League Club was founded by patriotic citizens whose primary purpose was to "cultivate a profound national devotion" and "to strengthen a love and respect for the Union."

The founders dedicated the Club as a civic forum for the frank discussion of public issues having these further aims:

"to dignify politics as a pursuit and as a study"

"to reawaken an active interest in civic affairs" and

"to enforce a sense of the sacred obligation of citizenship."

In the ensuing century, a great tradition of public service was established by the Club in which its members may well take pride today.

It is appropriate also that, in this Centennial year, we remind ourselves of the proud history of the Club and the distinguished achievements of the many public-spirited members with whom it has been identified.

It is appropriate also that, in these trying times, we look to the future and consider the ways in which the Club can perpetuate its traditional principles.

The year 1963 is therefore designated as "The Union League Club Centennial Year." The members are asked to join in the observance of this anniversary and to rededicate the Club to vigorous renewal of the faith and aims of the founders.

John C. Wood, President, by order of the Board of Governors

lunches, and the reprinting of the lengthy commemoration of the Club's forming the Colored Regiments during the Civil War. The Club also published a concise, illustrated narrative of its past titled *Highlights of History* in the Club's monthly *Bulletin*.

The Library played an important part in the celebration. No longer the sleepy retreat that Mr. Child had managed, it had an exhibit of books and artifacts of the Military Order of the Loyal Legion of the United States, an organization of Union Army commissioned officers founded by General Ulysses S. Grant. In January, two ceremonies honoring the opening of the Civil War were held at sites with close connections to the Club. A wreath was placed at the foot of the statue of Lincoln that Union League Club members had commissioned after his death and erected at Union Square. At Grant's Tomb, 1,200 West Point cadets and hundreds of other soldiers stood at attention under General Grant's famous saying, "Let Us Have Peace," and Club member Ulysses S. Grant III, chairman of the Civil War Centennial Commission, laid the first of four wreaths at the tomb of his grandfather.

One of the highlights of the centennial celebration was a long-playing record, *Story of a Century*, in which the Club's story and the music that accompanied it were blended, using the voices of the narrator and fifteen staff members who called themselves the Union League Club Chorus. These men had first sung together in December 1962 at the staff Christmas party (the first ever held at the Club). The group then made an impromptu appearance at a Board of Governors meeting, followed by a concert at the founders Day Luncheon, at which the Rev. Norman Vincent Peale was the lead speaker and commemorative medallions were presented to the Club's seventeen staff members who had been at the Club for fifty years or longer.

Thanks to Club member Peter M. Rogers, and led by musical director Joseph Bellow, the Chorus recorded "Story of a Century" at RCA-Victor Studios. The soloists were staff members William Ruff, Gifford Alesia, George H. Wiley, and Edwin L. Preswell. The narrator, Richard S. Stark, had one of the most unusual biographies of a Union League Club member. A child actor called

Dick Stark in silent movies, he served in the Marines in World War II, wrote novels, acted on the stage and in television, and was the announcer of *The Perry Como Kraft Music Show*, *What's My Line?*, and other television shows. An officer in the Marine Corps Reserves, Stark returned to active duty in 1966, served in Vietnam, and later was officer in charge of the Marine Corps' New York Information Office.[203]

Anybody expecting a dry lecture is immediately disarmed by the show's introduction. In the style of a typical daytime radio drama, organist William Meeder (a veteran of soap operas) softly plays "The Battle Hymn of the Republic" as Stark's mellifluous voice identifies the Union League and its projects with great people and institutions. The script, by Charles C. Coates, interweaves the Club's and country's histories with ten spirituals and patriotic songs performed by the Chorus. "Swing Low, Sweet Chariot" introduces the segment on slavery, "When Johnny Comes Marching Home" brings on the Civil War, the Spanish-American War is fought to "The Marine Corps Hymn," and so on to the closing, unifying rendition of "The Star Spangled Banner." Many members' names are mentioned in passing, from Thomas Nast to William Hayward to Honorary Member Dwight D. Eisenhower.

At the end of the recording, the story returns to the Club itself: "All honor to the founders," intones the narrator. "The vision they shared is a priceless legacy."[204]

The Club is well known for the views of the street below from comfortable chairs. This is Paul M. Ripley Treasurer in 1950-1954.

Dedication by General William Westmoreland of the plaque of Club members who served in Vietnam.

Plaque recognizing Club members who served in the hostilities in Vietnam.

Expanding Traditions

A few weeks after the end of the successful centennial celebration, President John C. Wood told his fellow members, "I, for one, believe firmly that our Club can have a future as fine as its past. But we must rededicate ourselves with vigor, sincerity and purpose to the great principles and traditions of the founders."[205] The Union League Club was undergoing challenges familiar to all clubs at that time. They were described in a *Time* magazine article, titled "Cold Wind in Clubland," that drew on a survey of the members and officials of fifty City clubs.

Opposite: *Ready for the Ride*
(William Merritt Chase, 1877)

Club members worked in New York, but most lived in the suburbs and spent most or all of their free time there. The post-war trends were eroding social distinctions, and upsetting a lifestyle that once seemed permanent. "At the turn of the century and on into the 'twenties," one club man told *Time*, "the things that were important were your school, your college, your club, the dances, trips to Europe, and where you went in the summer. Now all of these things are available to almost anyone and everyone—with one exception: the Club."[206] Clubs were unsure how to respond to these modern challenges to the traditional view that life is only as strong as its institutions. With expenses increasing more rapidly than income, even old-line clubs that had long been secure were considering mergers.

At the Union League Club, as the postwar membership boom slowed, the membership grayed. A member survey in 1960 revealed that one-half the members were sixty or older, and nearly one-third were over sixty-five. Similar problems had been uncovered by a previous member survey, in the 1920s. Back then, the Club had built a modern clubhouse with amenities to meet the new needs of its members. In 1964, it was unreasonable to expect the Club to build a new building, but old spaces could be put to new uses. The formerly sacrosanct Library was now available for parties and receptions and the Ladies Dining Room was enlarged.

The old admissions system was retained, with its "flower dance" choreography of placing candidates wearing white carnations at tables in the Grant Room, and rotating members of the Admissions Committee wearing red carnations. Yet much thought went into the new discipline called membership development. "The old members were upset that the Club felt it even had to have a Membership Development Committee and recruit new members," said E. Nicholson Stewart, who joined the Club in 1975 and was President from 1989 to 1991. The Club added a junior membership for members forty or younger, and a guest membership that allowed potential regular members to use the Club for three to six months before deciding to apply. In the 1990s, an option called the certificate program was introduced to help applicants with the initiation fee. Non-resident membership, which had been permitted in the early days, was retired during the membership boom, but was later revived. Eventually, a special non-resident membership category was developed for people who lived in remote parts of the country and who traveled to New York.

Women Members

When Floyd W. McKinnon (President, 2005–2007) was asked to identify the turning points in the Club's recent history, he named only one: "Taking the Club co-ed." There were women at the Club ever since it was founded, but never to the extent available beginning in 1988, when the Union League Club joined many other men's clubs in New York and around the country in accepting women as equal members. The road to this decision was long and winding.

In 1983, Mayor Ed Koch proposed Local Law 63, often called "the Private Clubs Bill," to the City Council. If it passed and survived the expected court challenges, the law would prohibit discrimination based on race, gender, or religion in clubs that were not "distinctly private." Under the proposed law, a club did not meet that standard if it had more than 400 members, offered regular meal service, and regularly received payments for services from non-members with the purpose of furthering business. "A club must regularly receive payments from outsiders to fall under this bill," explained the City's Corporation Counsel, F.A.O. Schwartz, Jr. "If people who belong to a club want to be biased, they ought to pay for it privately."[207]

Many, if not most, larger clubs in the City fit into the not distinctly private category because they depended at least to some extent on renting out space and services to non-members for lunches, banquets, cocktail parties, office parties, and business meetings. Sometimes a business rented a suite of rooms in a club for many days to conduct sensitive negotiations (in 1983, Braniff Airlines was reorganized from bankruptcy at the Union League Club). Commercial activity was so much a part of club life in those days that members who used a club for business were allowed to deduct the dues from their federal income taxes. Companies paying employees' dues were also entitled to a tax deduction. When the deduction was ended in the 1980s, most clubs lost members.

The "distinctly private" rule also targeted the indirect advantage of club membership known as networking, or developing social contacts for business purposes. "From an interpersonal standpoint it's wonderful," a man in the advertising business said of his Union League Club membership. "Friendships and the old boy network flourish."[208] Muriel Siebert, the first woman to hold a seat on the New York Stock Exchange, stressed the importance of networking: "For somebody coming up, to be able to join one of these clubs is super-imperative."[209]

Many clubs decided that it would be costly and futile to fight the Private Clubs Bill. Most changed their rules to permit women members, and a few opted to satisfy the "distinctly private" rule by barring business events in the Club that included non-members. Forty-seven other New York clubs, including the Union League Club, opted to oppose the Private Clubs Bill. Their argument was that there is an absolute and fundamental right to be able to select one's own friends in a private social setting. During a forum on the proposed law at the Association of the Bar of the City of New York, a lawyer opposed to the bill employed a domestic analogy: "I consider my club an extension of my home. What's the difference between discrimination that is allowed in my home, where I give a party for whomever I want and take a tax deduction, and discrimination at my club?"[210]

One of the counter-arguments was that clubs that do business with non-members are not, in fact, "distinctly private" institutions but "public accommodations" because they serve the broad public. Another argument was that the United States Supreme Court had already ruled that the government has a legitimate interest in infringing on free association in order to address concerns about racial, gender, and other discrimination.

In 1986, New York City's Commission on Human Rights initiated a formal complaint against the Union League Club, the Century Association, and the University Club, arguing that they were not "distinctly private." At the Union League Club, President A. Ted Quantz, Jr. (1986 to 1988) told the members that if the law were upheld, "The result would be that the Clubs would lose their ability to manage their own affairs, and admissions policies would, in effect, be handed over to City officials."[211] Quantz had been assured that his term as President would not be demanding. "I was told it would be an easy ride, two years and out," he said in an interview in 2000. The ride was not easy and it required another year. "The definitive issue of my three years," he said, was the fight over the Private Clubs Bill. At one time or another, the Club was a party to four legal actions—two in state courts, one before the Commission on Human Rights, and a suit that the Union League Club alone brought in federal court. The Club's endowment was small. House Committee Chairman William N. Otte, in his annual report, worried that Club projects would be affected by the cost of "defending our established position."[212]

The membership was torn. "When the issue of admitting women came up," John R. Farrington (Club President 2009–2012) said later, "some members said they would quit if women were going to be admitted, and other members said they'd quit if the rules weren't changed and their daughters couldn't get in." Although President Quantz believed that most members supported the Board's position, he declined to poll the membership out of concern that a survey would divide the members, as happened at another club. "That would have been asking for trouble," he said later.

Trouble was not easy to avoid, however. When the Board sent a questionnaire to the membership regarding the quality of Club service, some of the 700 members who responded changed the subject and inserted their rather fierce opinions about the Private Clubs Bill. (Quantz did learn that there was some frustration about dining room service. He took these frustrated replies to the staff and came away with a promise that anybody who was not served within twenty minutes of placing an order would get a refund.)

Asked later about the accomplishments of his three years as President, Quantz quickly replied, "Introducing women to the Club in a non-divisive way. The Board did that."

The Private Clubs Bill was upheld by two state lower courts and then by the New York State Court of Appeals. In addition, the Union League Club lost its federal case at the district level. The Club was waiting for its appeal to be heard when another appeal against the law reached the U.S. Supreme Court in February 1988, in *New York State Club Association, Inc.* v. *The City of New York.* In a unanimous decision by seven justices (the other two recused themselves because they were members of clubs with exclusionary membership rules), the Supreme Court ruled in favor of the New York law. Justice Byron R. White indicated in the Court's ruling that some clubs might be permitted to discriminate if they were formed primarily for religious or free-speech reasons, but only so long as there was no business or professional discussion at that club.

Federal law was settled, but there remained cases in New York courts. President Quantz wrote the members that, although he and the Board of Governors believed that the Union League Club had not violated any law, "as an expression of our loyalty" to the government and the Club's founding principle, the Board ended its fight against Local Law 63 in state courts. The Board passed the following resolution:

"RESOLVED that the Club will accept and consider applications submitted on behalf of women in the same manner and on the same basis as are accepted and considered on behalf of men, so that women may be admitted to full membership in the Club in accordance with all other admissions policies and procedures administered by the Club, and will treat women guests of members on the same basis as male guests of members; and it is further

RESOLVED that the House Committee is authorized to study the House Rules to implement the above resolution."[213]

In 1989, the Union League elected its first woman member, Faith Whittlesey Ryan, the Ambassador to Switzerland and a former advisor to President Ronald Reagan. Quantz would later say

that he was proud that he had brought about two firsts. He was the first Southerner to preside over the Union League Club and, he said, "I was the first President to open an Annual Meeting by saying 'lady and gentlemen.'" Soon it was "ladies" as other women joined.

The transition went successfully. Women members quietly assumed that the Main Bar was men's territory, and life went on there, as before. Marsha Malinowski's introduction to the Club was on the evening of September 11, 2001, when she was invited to dinner in the Mary Murray Room (the former Ladies Dining Room). "People started introducing themselves. It was very warm and welcoming, very enveloping." She applied for a guest membership "to see if it was a fit." Pleased with the experience, she was proposed for membership and was the only woman at

"Your Job"

A Club President during the first decade of women membership, Jack Orben, had a vivid experience with one woman at the Club.

"In my term, the Club awarded former Prime Minister Margaret Thatcher the Theodore Roosevelt American Experience Award. She arrived with two Scotland Yard agents and a personal assistant. I met her at the door and got her a drink and was telling her about the Club. I had to point out that because there were as yet no ladies rooms on the floor we were on, she would have to go upstairs. She looked at me and said, 'I lived through the blitz. Do you think I can't use a men's room?' Then as people began to crowd around us, she handed me her glass and told me, 'Your job is to hold my drink.'"

"That was a *very* special night."

the "flower dance" admissions meeting (where she met her husband). She became a member of the Board of Governors, was the first woman to serve on the Executive Committee, and chaired the History Committee.

No member was lost in the attacks on the World Trade Center, but hundreds, some covered in ashes, congregated at the Club. Televisions were set up in the Main Lounge, cell phones were allowed in the bar, and the staff put out food. Among the temporary refugees were Walter Lion and his wife and children, who had come into the City that morning for a dentist's appointment and, after the attacks, come over to the Club. "The Union League Club truly is my home away from home," said Lion. On September 11th, with the bedrooms quickly filling up, the Club gave the Lion family the Seward Room for their use as Lion hunted down diapers in the few stores that remained open on Murray Hill. When the bridges were finally opened, he drove his family back to the suburbs, and home.

The Club and Its Values

Ask members why they joined the Union League Club, and just about everyone will say that they were attracted by the Club's historic convictions. Jack Orben, Club President from 1997 to 1999, joined in 1984 because he respected the Club's values and looked up to the founders, whom he called, admiringly, "troublesome young men." Commenting in 2012 that the Club "remains a conservative flame for the members," he singled out the Committee on Public Affairs for introducing speakers and programs that make it "a home for like-minded people who share this point of view."

Opposite: *President George W. Bush*
(Everett Raymond Kinstler, 2012)

Club Presidents William Dreher, James McKinnon, John R. Farrington, James J. Jennings III, Richard Phelan, and Floyd W. McKinnon

A Club to Preserve the Union

Many members point to the Civil War as the Club's touchstone. Said Mary Beth Sullivan, "I love the story of the founding, including a Founding Father's grandson, John Jay. I am proud of what this Club has done to support the country, its support of Lincoln and the Union cause, of its recruitment of the black regiments, and its efforts to bring the Statue of Liberty to New York."

Club President David Mathus recounts, "Our Club was formed in February and March of 1863 by many of the leading citizens of New York to sustain the Union. The founders included the grandsons of many of the Republic's early leaders, including the grandsons of John Jay, Roger Sherman, and Oliver Wolcott. Since

Past and present members of Board of Governors, 2012

The Tapp Foundation

Floyd W. "Wink" McKinnon joined the Club in 1967 and served as President from 2005 to 2007. Neither he nor his brother James President 1995–1997) had to be lured into joining because their father was a member. A total of six McKinnons have been members at one time or another. "My dad loved this Club," Wink McKinnon said. "He lived and breathed this Club. When he retired to North Carolina, he missed it." His brother Jim added, "The Club is one of the only bastions of conservatism in New York, 'a red island in a blue universe.'"

Wink McKinnon worked with former President E. Nicholson Stewart (1989 to 1991) and others in raising and distributing money for the Robert Hampton Tapp Foundation. Founded in 1994, and named for a much admired Club President who died in 1991, the Tapp Foundation's primary concern is providing financial assistance for the education of children of the Union League Club's employees. About $50,000 is raised for the Tapp Foundation every year through the Members' Christmas Party, the Annual Book Fair, other Club events, and contributions.

President Theodore Roosevelt
(George Burroughs Torrey, 1905)
"Make him mad," Torrey was advised before his first sitting with Roosevelt.
"You'll get him best that way."

President William Howard Taft
(George Burroughs Torrey, 1909)
President Taft is one of nine public officials whose portraits were painted
by George Burroughs Torrey and are displayed at the Club.

our founding, the Club and its members, including Presidents and Justices, have played significant roles in the nation's history."

When former President James Jennings (2012 to 2013) was asked, "What does the Club stand for?" he replied, "Our principles today parallel what we held in 1863. We have the same articles of association. We have the same attitudes about assuming civic duties. We have the same long list of accomplishments. We are equally respectful and supportive of the armed services.

President Calvin Coolidge
(Wayman Adams, 1931)
President Coolidge's New England heritage is a feature of his portrait,
displayed in the Main Lounge alongside other presidential portraits.

President Herbert Hoover
(George Burroughs Torrey, 1929)
A staff member who was at the Club for sixty years served every
Republican President from Benjamin Harrison to Herbert Hoover.

Our members have served in every conflict from the Civil War to Vietnam, Iraq, and Afghanistan and we continue to honor veterans of our armed forces at the Union League Clubhouse."

The military has long received the Club's allegiance and respect.

"I feel humble and privileged when sitting under the portraits of Grant, Sherman, and Sheridan in the Grant Room," Walter Lion has said.

Of the Club's twelve Honorary Members in 1889, seven were retired generals or admirals. As of 2012, a large proportion of the

James A. Trowbridge
(George Burroughs Torrey)
These men were of the old order, before world wars and the Depression.
James A. Trowbridge was a New York banker.

Samuel W. Fairchild
(George Burroughs Torrey)
Club President Samuel W. Fairchild (1911-14) established the Club's
leadership role regarding Preparedness.

nearly 200 Honorary Members continue to be military officers. Friendly relations with the military continue today. The close relationship with West Point, for example, includes an annual trap shoot competition at the Academy after a formal dinner at the Club, with the cadets in dress whites, and the regular appearances at the Club by the United States Military Academy Glee Club. Other military-related events honored by the Club include the Memorial Day wreath-laying, the celebration of the birthday of

Charles Evans Hughes
(George Burroughs Torrey)
Club President Charles Evans Hughes (1917-19) was New York governor
and Chief Justice of the U.S. Supreme Court.

Joseph H. Choate
(Herbert Adams)
Club President Joseph H. Choate (1873-76) prosecuted the Tweed Ring
and served as Ambassador to Great Britain.

the Marine Corps, receptions for winners of the Congressional Medal of Honor, and the appearances of honor guards. When the planning committee for the 2012 NYC Veterans' Day Parade met, it was at the Club.

Presidents and Their Portraits

The Union League Club's 150-year history of close relationships with the military and the White House are represented in the art collections of the Club as well. There are Civil War battlefield

Chauncey M. Depew (President, 1886-92)
(George Burroughs Torrey, 1921)

Chief Justice, U.S. Supreme Court, Warren Burger
(Jacob Collins, 1980)

scenes, and also the long line of portraits of Republican Presidents of the United States. Each Republican President has been an Honorary Member of the Club and, with the exception of Warren Harding, are all represented by at least one work of art at the Club.

The story of the Club and the Presidents begins in 1863 with the man in whose cause the Club was founded, and who was the Club's first Honorary Member—Abraham Lincoln. Founder George Templeton Strong called him "our great and good President." The Club is not only well known for its collection of Lincoln-related art works, but also for the commission and donation of the statue of Lincoln, sculpted by Henry Kirke Brown, that stands in Union Square. In 2010, the History Committee placed

President Richard Nixon
(Everett Raymond Kinstler, 1985)

President Gerald R. Ford
(Everett Raymond Kinstler, 1978)

a new plaque on the statue through the generosity of member Douglas Wyatt.

Another President with whom the Club was closely connected is Ulysses S. Grant. The Union League helped create his memorial on Riverside Drive, and his portrait hangs in the Grant Room with other Civil War generals. Two Presidents were Club members before they went to the White House—Chester Arthur and Theodore Roosevelt. In addition to painting Theodore Roosevelt, George Burroughs Torrey painted portraits of three other United States' Presidents, Calvin Coolidge, Herbert Hoover, and

William Howard Taft, all of which hang in the Club. It was Taft who advised Torrey that he must accurately show Taft's stomach because "I've been all my life getting it and I'm proud of it." Torrey also painted portraits of Club Presidents Joseph H. Choate, Chauncey M. Depew, Samuel W. Fairchild, Charles Evans Hughes, and Charles Cook Paulding, and of member James A. Trowbridge.

Presidents Grant, Arthur, Theodore Roosevelt, Hoover, Eisenhower, Nixon, and George H. W. Bush frequented the Club. After leaving office in 1932 and until his death in 1964, Hoover often

Passing the Outpost
(A. Wordsworth Thompson, 1881)

took meals at the Club and participated in Club activities. Long before Eisenhower was elected President in 1952, he was elected as an Honorary Member while he wore the uniform as U.S. Army Chief of Staff. He and his advisors came to the Club often when he was a presidential candidate and during his eight years in office. Once when he was at the Club to give a talk in 1963, he expressed so much affection for the luncheon roast beef that the Club took an entire roast from its larder and sent it to the President at his home near Gettysburg.

President Reagan sent this note of thanks to the Club when *Passing the Outpost* and *Preaching to the Troops* were returned by the White House.

Seventh Regiment Encampment Near Washington
Sanford Robinson Gifford enlisted for three summers with the New York Seventh Regiment, mostly guarding Washington and
Baltimore. Gifford saw active duty only when the Seventh Regiment was recalled to New York City to quell the draft riots in July 1863.
The four paintings he made of his army service focus on quiet moments of reflection rather than the action of war.
(Sanford Robinson Gifford)

The Union League Club Art Selections at the White House

The Club is connected with the White House through the Union League's art collection. In 1974 the Club loaned two paintings to the White House to be displayed in the office of Vice President Nelson Rockefeller. These paintings were *Passing the Outpost*, an historical scene from the Revolutionary War by A. Wordsworth Thompson, and a landscape by Childe Hassam, *Connecticut Landscape*.

The landscape was returned to the Union League Club in January 1976, and replaced in the White House by one of the finest works in the Club's collection, an oil painting titled *Seventh Regiment Encampment Near Washington* by Club member Sanford Robinson Gifford. Painted in the early days of the war, it portrays a sweeping view from the heights of Arlington across the Potomac to the city. The viewer's eye quickly focuses on a man wrapped in the American flag as he preaches to a group of uniformed soldiers who are members of New York's Seventh Regiment. Often called *Preaching to the Troops*, this arresting painting reflects the Union League Club's support of the war.

To The Union League Club, in appreciation of your wonderful cooperation and thoughtfulness. With warmest best wishes. Jerry Ford

When the White House returned *Landscape with Trees* to the Club, this photograph and a note by President Ford were sent as well.

Soon after Gifford's exquisite painting, *Seventh Regiment Encampment Near Washington,* arrived at the White House in 1976, the curator wrote the Club to say that it had quickly become "an instant favorite at the White House among all who have seen it." When it and *Passing the Outpost* were returned to the Club twelve years later, President Ronald Reagan wrote to Club President Albert T. "Ted" Quantz " . . . They've been a real pleasure to have in the Oval Office and I've always pointed them out to visitors. I hate to admit it, but I'm going to miss them."

The history of these paintings continues to be enriched.

Landscape with Trees (Orchard in Summer)
(Childe Hassam)

In 2012 to 2013, *Seventh Regiment Encampment Near Washington* was included in a year-long exhibition titled "The Civil War and American Art," jointly curated by the Smithsonian American Art Museum and the Metropolitan Museum of Art. Since 2008, a reproduction of *Seventh Regiment Encampment Near Washington*, with the Club's permission, has been on permanent exhibit in Washington, D.C., at President Lincoln's Cottage, a house in which the Lincoln family lived for several months each year.

Honoring Presidents Reagan and Bush

When former President Reagan came to the Club in 1990 to accept an Honorary Membership, he was presented with a bust of Abraham Lincoln by Club President E. Nicholson Stewart. The ceremony began with an invocation by the Rev. Norman Vincent Peale with music provided by the U.S. Air Force Band of the East. Several years later, in 1999, President Reagan's portrait, by Charles Fagan, was unveiled in the Main Lounge with a tribute given by former Attorney General Edwin Meese. Shown in the background of the Club's portrait of President Ronald Reagan is Thompson's *Passing the Outpost*, the painting he enjoyed so much during his presidency.

The Club's close association with President Reagan continued long after his death. In 2012 his alma mater, Eureka College, chose the Club as the site of its Reagan Fellowship Award Dinner, honoring James A. Baker III, Reagan's Chief of Staff. Held in March, this event was attended by many surviving members of the Reagan administration as well as by many Club members.

President Reagan's successor, George H.W. Bush, visited the Club many times, beginning in 1971 when he was Ambassador to the United Nations. He was present when his portrait was unveiled in 1994, with the Armed Forces Color Guard in full regalia. When President Bush was presented with the Club's Theodore Roosevelt American Experience Award in 1996, he was introduced by General Brent Scowcroft, National Security Advisor during the Bush administration, and the White House Color Guard and United States Military Academy Glee Club participated in the ceremony.

President Ronald Reagan
(Nelson Shanks, 1989)

On another occasion, in 2002, President Bush, by then an Honorary Member, shared recollections of his World War II military service and enthusiastically engaged with the other veterans and spectators at the Club's History Committee event honoring members who were veterans of World War II. Assistant Manager

President Bush during the Republican National Convention at Madison Square Garden.

History Revived

In the late 1980s, a new level of interest in the Club's history was brought about by the coincidence of the Statue of Liberty's centennial in 1986 and the Club's 125th anniversary in 1988. President Ted Quantz, together with a group of Club members who were interested in the Club's identity and heritage, were a catalyst for all that followed. "These events were so meaningful to the Club," said Quantz, "we decided it would be a perfect time to educate the members about the rich heritage of the Club." This history came to life for Quantz and other members when the chairman of the committee restoring the Statue, Lee Iacocca, spoke at the Union League Club. The Club hosted a reception for captains of the tall ships and other vessels that took part in the international naval review honoring the Statue in New York Harbor, and many members were aboard the aircraft carrier *John F. Kennedy* to watch the parade of ships that day. Chief Justice Warren Burger was the main speaker at the Club's 125th anniversary.

After the Club founded the History Committee in 1997, its Chairman, Richard P. Phelan, began writing his "History Corner" column for publication in the *Bulletin* with accounts of the cartoonist Thomas Nast and of Colonel William Hayward and the Fifteenth Regiment (Colored). Another sixty-four more "History Corner" articles followed over the next six years. Besides stories and biographies about important events and people, Phelan passed on historical tidbits such as the fact that the Club President's gavel is made from the wood of an elm tree planted by Daniel Webster, and the gavel block is from the original hull of the USS *Constitution*.[205]

A man of considerable energy and deep devotion to the Union League Club and its history, Richard Phelan led the History Committee in honoring Barbara Bush as " . . . only the second woman to be both the wife and the mother of Presidents" (the other is Abigail Adams). Mrs. Bush was so taken with her portrait by Chas

President George H. W. Bush
(Jacob Collins, 1994)

Janet Ryder spoke for many people who were present on that occasion when she said, "This was one of the most emotional events I've ever attended."

The Bush family stayed at the Club that night and at many other times. In 2004, forty rooms were reserved at the Club for

First Lady Barbara Bush
(Chas Fagan, 2004)

Fagan, which Club members had commissioned, that she asked if she could keep it for the White House. The Club had another portrait painted and it now hangs in the Mary Murray Lounge.

Honoring History

During Club History Month in 1999, the History Committee revived an old Club tradition of holding a dinner in February commemorating both Lincoln's birthday and the anniversary of the Club's founding. Club President Jack Orben opened the 1999 dinner with a toast to President Lincoln with an 1863 Boal's Madeira. Over the years, the History Committee welcomed David McCullough, Ken Burns, Harold Holzer, and Karl Rove, among others, as the featured speaker for this dinner. In 2008, the Committee featured Club member Ray Price, who spoke about his years of working with President Nixon. Three months later, President Eisenhower's role in the D-Day landing was the topic of a talk by his grandson, David Eisenhower.

Other speakers in recent years have included former Cabinet ministers, presidential assistants or advisors, and many other government and military leaders. From 2011 to 2012, Public Affairs and Military Affairs speakers who addressed the membership included the governors of New Jersey, Virginia, Mississippi, and Wisconsin; the Majority Leader of the U.S. House of Representatives and the most senior Republican members of the U.S. Senate; the Air Force Chief of Staff, the Commandant of the Coast Guard, and numerous and other current and former government and military leaders.

The Club's traditional Memorial Day ceremony begins with a wreath-laying by a senior military officer and ends with a black-tie dinner.

Awards for Accomplishment

The Club presents four awards for accomplishment: The Eastman Johnson Award, presented by the Art Committee; the American History Award, presented by the History Committee; the Lincoln Literary Award, presented by the Library Committee; and the Theodore Roosevelt American Experience Award, presented by the Committee on Public Affairs. The Committees nominate candidates for their awards, and present their recommendations to the Board of Governors for final selection. The first Theodore Roosevelt Award was presented in 1995 to General Brent Scowcroft, a well-known and respected foreign policy authority. Subsequent awards have been presented to former President George H.W. Bush and former Prime Minister Margaret Thatcher, among others.

A Contested Election

In 2007, the first contested election for Club officers since 1890 took place. In accordance with the Club's bylaws, Richard Phelan headed an alternate slate that ran against the Nominating Committee's choice for officers, Board of Governors, and Admissions Committee nominees. Differences of opinion had developed over the years preceding the election regarding admissions, appointment of committees, and communications in the Club. Election night brought a great many interested and concerned members to the Club to mark their ballots. Candidates from both the Nominating Committee and the alternative slates were elected, and Richard Phelan was elected President. It was a chapter in the history of the Union League Club that demonstrated the great care all its members have for the welfare and the leadership of the Club.

After 150 years of hosting soldiers and sailors, the Club knows how to do it very well. The Achilles Freedom Team of Wounded Veterans came in 2012.

The Hope and Possibility Road Race in Central Park was a centerpiece of the Achilles Team's activities in New York City.

2012: A Spring Full of Honors

The Club's historic relationships with both the military and the Presidency of the United States coincided with three striking and important events that took place in late May and early June of 2012. They were the Memorial Day Wreath Hanging, the annual visit of the Achilles Freedom Team of Wounded Veterans, and a visit by a former President of the United States.

The Memorial Day ceremony is one of the Club's most moving events, with a wreath-laying by a senior military officer followed by a black-tie dinner. In 2012, the wreath was laid by the Commandant of the United States Coast Guard, Admiral Robert J. Papp, Jr., and a painting of the Coast Guard Cutter *Katherine Walker* was presented to the Club from the Coast Guard's

permanent art collection. The ceremony featured the reading of the citation for awarding the Bronze Star to Club President James Jennings' father, who was wounded in World War II.

Two weeks after Memorial Day in 2012, the Club hosted forty disabled soldiers and their guests for the five-mile Hope and Possibility Road Race in Central Park. Patients at Walter Reed National Military Medical Center, in Bethesda, Maryland, these veterans were members of the Achilles Freedom Team of Wounded Veterans, founded in 2004 and sponsored by Achilles International.

Beginning in 2006, the Club hosted runners and their guests for the weekend in New York. The 2012 trip included a Yankees-Mets baseball game, a police escort through the City, a speedboat ride on the Hudson, and a visit to Ground Zero, where the

The week in the city also included a visit to Ground Zero, where the veterans were honored by a gathering of first responders.

All who met the forty members of the Achilles Team who stayed at the Club with their families were deeply moved by their courage.

runners were greeted by a group of 9/11 first responders[206] standing at attention. "If that doesn't grip your heart, there's something missing," said President Jennings, in reaction to the Ground Zero event.

The third of the patriotic events that occupied the Union League Club in the spring of 2012 was the arrival on June 13th of former President George W. Bush, accompanied by his wife, Laura. His portrait was unveiled by the artist in Lincoln Hall and President Bush was awarded the Club's Theodore Roosevelt American Experience Award. In his comments, President Bush cited the long, exemplary history of military service by American citizens, at personal risk to themselves.

These events on the eve of the Union League Club's 150th

Anniversary carries on the Club's long tradition of honoring the nation's history, motivated by values that have been at the core of the Club's identity since the time the founders stepped forward during the dark days of 1863 and volunteered "to enforce a sense of the sacred obligation inherent in citizenship."

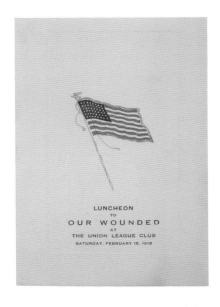

LUNCHEON
TO
OUR WOUNDED
AT
THE UNION LEAGUE CLUB
SATURDAY, FEBRUARY 15, 1919

Program for the luncheon for wounded soldiers held at the Club February 15, 1919.

President George W. Bush admires his portrait after its unveiling at the Club in June 2012

Honorary Members 1965–2013

Honorary Member	Elected to Honorary Membership	Admitted to Regular Membership (if applicable)	Notable Achievements
Thomas Weldon Dunn	1965		Lieutenant General, United States Army
John S. McCain, Jr.	1965		Admiral, United States Navy
Andrew McBurney Jackson, Jr.	1967		Vice Admiral, United States Navy
Charles Marsden Duke	1968		Major General, United States Army
Osmund A. Leahy	1968		Major General, United States Army
Alfred M. Gruenther	1969		General, United States Army
Arnold Frederick Schade	1970		Vice Admiral, United States Navy
Louis J. Schelter, Jr.	1971		Brigadier General, United States Army
Richard G. Stilwell	1971		General, United States Army
B. F. Engel	1971		Rear Admiral, United States Coast Guard
Harry L. Harty, Jr.	1971		Vice Admiral, United States Navy
Austin J. Russell	1971		Lieutenant General, United States Air Force
J. Nevin Shaffer	1971		Rear Admiral, United States Navy
John M. Hightower	1972		Major General, United States Army
Witham M. Pugh	1972		Rear Admiral, United States Navy
Durward L. Crow	1973		Lieutenant General, United States Air Force
Joseph P. Moorer	1973		Vice Admiral, United States Navy
William F. Rea, III	1974		Vice Admiral, United States Coast Guard
Marion L. Boswell	1974		Lieutenant General, United States Air Force
Frank B. Guest, Jr.	1975		Rear Admiral, United States Naval Reserve
Robert I. Price	1978		Vice Admiral, United States Coast Guard
Gerald R. Ford	1978 and 1980		President of the United States
James L. Buckley	1981		United States Senator
William Casey	1981		Director, Central Intelligence Agency
E. Pendleton James	1981	1978	Assistant to the President for Presidential Personnel
P. Thomas Cantrell	1983		
James S. Gracey	1981		Admiral, Commandant of United States Coast Guard
Frank Shakespeare	1985 and 1990		United States Ambassador to Portugal and the Holy See
Nicholas J. Mertens	1987		
Warren Burger	1988		United States Supreme Court Chief Justice
Ronald Reagan	1988		President of the United States
Edwin C. McDonald	1994	1964	President, Union League Club
George H. W. Bush	1994		President of the United States
Albert Reynolds	1994		Prime Minister of Ireland; negotiated the settlement with the IRA and was nominated for the Nobel Peace Prize
Henry A. Kissinger	1995		United States Secretary of State
Brent Scowcroft	1997		United States National Security Advisor
Margaret Thatcher	1997		The Right Honorable The Baroness Thatcher, LG, OM, PC
Caspar W. Weinberger	1997		United States Secretary of Defense
H. Norman Schwarzkopf	2000		General, United States Army
Sandra Day O'Connor	2004		United States Supreme Court Justice
Barbara Bush	2005		First Lady of the United States
Neil A. Armstrong	2007		Mission Commander, National Aeronautics and Space Administration (NASA)
Antonin Scalia	2007		United States Supreme Court Justice
Peter Pace	2008		General, United States Marine Corps, Chairman, Joint Chiefs of Staff, United States Armed Forces
David Petraeus	2009		General, United States Army, Director, Central Intelligence Agency
Edwin Eugene "Buzz" Aldrin, Jr.	2011		Colonel, United States Air Force
George W. Bush	2012		President of the United States
Raymond T. Ordierno	2013		General, United States Army Chief of Staff of the United States Army

The Eastman Johnson Award

The Eastman Johnson Award, created in 2001, is presented to individuals whose unique contributions to art and culture have elevated the ideals of American Citizenship.

2001   Dr. John Wilmerding, the Christopher B. Sarophim Professor in American art and chair of art at the Metropolitan Museum of Art.

2005   Chas Fagan, the prominent American portrait artist, landscape painter and sculptor whose work is found in venues including the White House, National Cathedral, and our own Club.

2007   Everett Raymond Kinstler, one of the nation's foremost portrait artists and whose work includes more than 50 Cabinet officers and six Presidents from Richard Nixon to George W. Bush.

The American History Award

The Union League Club American History Award is presented to an individual who has had a significant impact on American History. The recipient, chosen with the unanimous approval of the History committee and Board of Governors, may come from any of a number of fields, including policitcs, the military, literature, journalism economics and education. The recipient is a person who we wish to recognize for his or her special contribution either to the making of our American story or for adding to the understanding of our common past. Above all else, the recipient of this Award has enriched our Nation's legacy. The Award is meant to reflect the rich traditions of the Club and its support of American ideals.

2003   Ken Burns

2004   Brian Lamb

2005   William F. Buckley, Jr.

2007   James McPherson

2007   David McCullough

2008   Victor Davis Hanson

2009   John Lewis Gaddis

2010   Edwin Eugene "Buzz" Aldrin, Jr.

2013   Richard Brookhiser

The Abraham Lincoln Literary Award

The award is in recognition of the author's outstanding contribution to American literature.

1977	Irwin Shaw		1992	Michael Crichton
1978	James Mitchener		1993	David McCullough
1979	Louis Auchincloss		1994	Joyce Carol Oates
1980	John Chever		1995	Henry A Kissinger
1981	Alistair Cooke		1996	David Herbert Donald
1982	John Updike		1998	Stephen E. Ambrose
1983	William Manchester		2000	Ron Chernow
1984	Barbara Tuchman		2001	P. J. O'Rourke
1985	William F. Buckley Jr.		2002	William Kennedy
1986	Neil Simon		2003	Thomas Fleming
1987	Tom Clancy		2004	George Will
1988	Brendan Gill		2005	Peggy Noonan
1989	Garrison Keillor		2006	James Salter
1990	Tom Wolfe		2007	Mark Bouden
1991	George Plimpton			

Theodore Roosevelt American Experience Award

Since the founding of the Union League Club in 1863 to support the Union cause in the Civil War, public affairs have been a major focus of its activities. The Theodore Roosevelt American Experience Award, established in 1994, is presented by the club, on the recommendation of the Public Affairs Committee, to a national or international figure in recognition of "outstanding service or accomplishment that in a uniquely significant way has enriched the American Experience or exemplified the American ideal."

In presenting the award, the Club recognizes that the American Experience is roted in the unique nature of the United States as the one nation drawn from all nations and as a beacon of hope to the world. It also recognizes that the experience takes diverse forms and is expressed in many ways—from science to statecraft and from industry to the arts.

The Award is named for the 26th President of the United States, who was also one of the Club's most eminent and active members. War hero, reformer, trustbuster, outdoorsman and prolific author, Theodore Roosevelt epitomizes the spirit of the people of the United States of America.

1995	Lt. General Brent Scowcroft, USAF (Ret.)
1996	President George H. W. Bush
1997	The Baroness Thatcher
2000	General H. Norman Schwarzkopf, USA (Ret.)
2002	Senator John S. McCain, III
2003	Justice Sandra Day O'Connor
2006	Justice Antonin G. Scalia
2006	Commander Neil A. Armstrong, USN (Ret.)
2008	General Peter Pace, USMC (Ret.)
2009	Dr. Henry A. Kissinger
2012	President George W. Bush

Sports

Special Events

Club Events

Festivities

Anniversary

150

1863

Staff

Selected Bibliography

Research for this book was conducted in the libraries of the Union League Club, the Century Association, Columbia University, and Union Theological Seminary, and at the New York Public Library and the Greenwich, Connecticut Public Library.

Histories of the Union League Club

Bellows, Henry W. *Historical Sketch of the Union League Club of New York: Its Origin, Organization, and Work, 1863-1879.* New York: Union League Club, 1879.

Coates, Charles C. and Richard S. Stark. *Story of a Century.* Recording. New York: Union League Club /RCA-Victor, 1963.

Highlights of History. New York: Union League Club, 1963.

Irwin, Will, Earl Chapman May, and Joseph Hotchkiss. *A History of the Union League Club of New York City.* New York: Dodd, Mead, 1952.

Phelan, Richard P. "History Corner" columns. Union League Club *Bulletin,* 1999-2004.

Union League Club *Yearbook,* 1864-2011.

Union League Club Clubhouses

Holden, Wheaton Arnold. *Robert Swain Peabody of Peabody and Stearns in Boston, the Early Years (1870-1886).* Boston University, Ph.D. dissertation, 1969.

Postal, Matthew A. "Union League Club," Landmarks Preservation Commission report October 25, 2011. http://www.nyc.gov/html/lpc/downloads/pdf/reports/2389.pdf

Stern, Robert A. M., Thomas Mellins, and David Fishman. *New York 1880: Architecture and Urbanism in the Gilded Age.* New York: Monacelli, 1999.

Stern, Robert A. M., Gregory Gilmartin, and Thomas Mellins. *New York 1930: Architecture and Urbanism between the Two World Wars.* New York: Rizzoli, 1987.

The Union League Club Members

Day, Clarence. *Life with Father.* New York: Knopf, 1935.

Depew, Chauncey. *My Memories of Eighty Years.* New York: Scribner, 1922.

Hayward, William. "A Tribute to My French General," *North American Review.* January-June 1919.

Jessup, Philip C. *Elihu Root.* 2 vols. New York: Dodd, Mead, 1938.

Kring, Walter Donald. *Henry Whitney Bellows.* Boston: Skinner House, 1979.

Morris, Edmund. *Colonel Roosevelt.* New York: Random House, 2010.

---*The Rise of Theodore Roosevelt.* New York: Coward, McCann & Geoghegan, 1979.

---*Theodore Rex.* New York: Random House, 2001.

Paine, Albert Bigelow. *Th. Nast: His Period and His Pictures.* New York: Macmillan, 1904.

Pringle, Henry F. *The Life and Times of William Howard Taft.* New York: Farnum and Rinehart, 1932.

Pusey, Merlo J. *Charles Evans Hughes.* New York: Macmillan, 1951.

Roosevelt, Theodore. *Autobiography.* New York: Macmillan, 1913.

Roper, Laura Wood. *FLO: A Biography of Frederick Law Olmsted.* Baltimore, Johns Hopkins University Press, 1973.

Strouse, Jean. *Morgan: American Financier.* New York: Random House, 1999.

Strong, George Templeton. *Diary.* Ed. Allan Nevins and Milton Halsey Thomas. 4 vols. New York: Macmillan, 1952.

-----. *Diary of the Civil War, 1860-1865.* Ed. Allan Nevins. New York: Macmillan, 1962.

Strong, Theron George. *Joseph H. Choate: New Englander, New Yorker, Lawyer, Ambassador.* New York: Dodd Mead, 1917.

Zachs, Richard. *Island of Vice: Theodore Roosevelt's Doomed Quest to Clean Up Sin-Loving New York.* New York: Doubleday, 2012.

New York History

Albion, Robert Greenhalgh. *Rise of New York Port, 1815-1860*. New York: Scribner's, 1939.

Barratt, Carrie Rebora. "*Washington Crossing the Delaware* and the Metropolitan Museum." *The Metropolitan Museum of Art Bulletin*, Fall 2012, 5-19.

Burrows, Edwin G. and Mike Wallace. *Gotham: A History of New York City to 1898*. New York: Oxford University Press, 1999.

Hammack, David C. *Power and Society: Greater New York at the Turn of the Century*. New York: Columbia University Press, 1982.

Hone, Philip. *The Diary of Philip Hone, 1828-1851*. New York: Dodd, Mead, 1927.

Jackson, Kenneth, ed. *Encyclopedia of New York City*. 2nd ed. New Haven: Yale University Press, 2010.

Rousmaniere, John. *Green Oasis in Brooklyn: The Evergreens Cemetery, 1849-2008*. Kittery ME: Seapoint Books, 2008.

Rozenzweig, Roy and Elizabeth Blackmar. *The Park and the People: A History of Central Park*. Ithaca: Cornell University Press, 1992.

Tompkins, Calvin. *Merchants and Masterpieces: The Story of the Metropolitan Museum of Art*. New York: Holt, 1989.

The Civil War

Bellows, Henry W. *Unconditional Loyalty*. New York: Edward O. Jenkins, 1863.

Bernstein, Iver. *The New York City Draft Riots: Their Significance for American Society and Politics in the Age of the Civil War*. New York: Oxford University Press, 1990.

----. "The Volcano under the City." *State of the Union: New York and the Civil War*. Ed. Harold Holzer. New York: Fordham University Press, 2002.

Fairfield, Francis Gerry. *Clubs of New York, With an Account of the Origin, Progress, Present Condition, and Membership of the Leading Clubs; an Essay on New York Club-Life, and Photographs of Leading Club-Men*. New York: Hinton, 1873.

Frederickson, George. *The Inner Civil War*. New York: Harper, 1965.

Schechter, Barnet. *The Devil's Own Work: The New York Draft Riots and the Fight to Reconstruct America*. New York: Walker, 2005.

Williams, George Washington. *A History of the Negro Troops in the War of the Rebellion, 1861-1865*, New York: Harper & Brothers, 1887.

Politics

Ackerman, Kenneth D. *Boss Tweed: The Rise and Fall of the Corrupt Pol Who Conceived the Soul of Modern New York*. Berkley: Carroll & Graf, 2006.

Asbury, Herbert. *The Gangs of New York: An Informal History of the Underworld* (orig. publ. 1937). New York: Random House Digital, 2008.

Callow, Alexander B., Jr. *The Tweed Ring*. New York: Oxford University Press, 1965.

Kyvig, David E. *Repealing National Prohibition*. Chicago: University of Chicago Press, 1979.

Ranus, Shelly A. "Constitutional Law: New York State Club Association v. City of New York." *Marquette Law Review*. Vol. 72, no. 3 (Spring 1989).

World War I

Badger, Reid. *Life in Ragtime: A Biography of James Reese Europe*. New York: Oxford University Press, 1995.

Barbeau, Arthur E. and Florette Henri. *The Unknown Soldiers: Black American Troops in World War I*. Philadelphia: Temple University Press, 1974.

Davison, Henry Pomeroy. *The American Red Cross in the Great War*. New York: Macmillan, 1919.

Harris, Stephen L. *Harlem's Hell Fighters: The African-American 369th Infantry in World War I*. Washington: Brassey, 2003.

Lamont, Thomas W. *Henry P. Davison: The Record of a Useful Life*. New York: Harper, 1933.

Little, Arthur W. *From Harlem to the Rhine: The Story of New York's Volunteers*. New York: Covici Friede, 1936.

Endnotes

1. George Frederickson, *The Inner Civil War* (New York: Harper & Row, 1965), 98.

2. Walter Donald Kring, *Henry Whitney Bellows* (Boston: Skinner House, 1979), 11.

3. George B. Kauffman, "Oliver Wolcott Gibbs," *American National Biography*, vol. 8, 925.

4. Henry W. Bellows, "Cities and Parks: with Special Reference to the New York Central Park," *Atlantic*, Apr. 1861.

5. Kring, *Henry Whitney Bellows*, 231.

6. Kring, *Henry Whitney Bellows*, 245.

7. Laura Wood Roper, *FLO: A Biography of Frederick Law Olmsted* (Baltimore, Johns Hopkins University Press, 1973), 169, 189.

8. *The United States Sanitary Commission: A Sketch of its Purpose and its Work* (Boston: Little, Brown, 1863), 20. George Templeton Strong, *Diary of the Civil War*, 1860-1865, ed. Allan Nevins (New York: Macmillan, 1962), 218.

9. Strong, *Diary of the Civil War*, 580, 587, 589.

10. Kring, *Henry Whitney Bellows*, 233.

11. Abraham Lincoln, *Collected Works of Abraham Lincoln*, ed. Roy P. Basler (Springfield, Ill.: Abraham Lincoln Association, 1955), vol. 4, 543.

12. Henry W. Bellows, *Historical Sketch of the Union League Club of New York: Its Origin, Organization, and Work, 1863-1879* (New York: Union League Club, 1879), 5.

13. *Memorial to LeGrand B. Cannon* (New York: Union League Club), 1906, 4, 17.

14. Henry Clews, *Address at a Reception Given by the Members on the Occasion of the Fiftieth Anniversary of the Founding of the Union League Club* (New York: Union League Club, 1913).

15. Henry W. Bellows, *Unconditional Loyalty* (New York: Edward O. Jenkins, 1863), 12.

16. Richard McKay, *South Street: A Maritime History of New York* (New York: Putnam's, 1934), 122.

17. Robert Greenhalgh Albion, *Rise of New York Port, 1815-1860* (New York: Scribner's, 1939). 86.

18. James Crosby Brown, *A Hundred Years of Merchant Banking, a History of Brown Brothers and Company* (Boston: Brown Brothers and Company, 1909), 290.

19. Iver Bernstein, *The New York City Draft Riots: Their Significance for American Society and Politics in the Age of the Civil War* (New York: Oxford University Press, 1990), 151.

20. Strong, *Diary of the Civil War*, 575.

21. George Templeton Strong, *Diary*, ed. Allan Nevins and Milton Halsey Thomas (New York: Macmillan, 1952), vol. 4, 35.

22. John Jay, "America Free or America Slave: An Address on the State of the Country," New York Tribune. 1856. http://archive.org/details/americafreeorame00jayj

23. Theron George Strong, *Joseph H. Choate: New Englander, New Yorker, Lawyer, Ambassador* (New York: Dodd Mead, 1917), 101.

24. Will Irwin, Earl Chapman May, and Joseph Hotchkiss, *A History of the Union League Club of New York* City (New York: Dodd, Mead, 1952), 246.

25. *Memorial to LeGrand B. Cannon*, 4, 17.

26. Report from Russell Flinchum, Archivist, Century Association.

27. Bellows, *Historical Sketch*, 21-2.

28. Theodore Roosevelt, *New York* (London: Longmans Green, 1891), 211.

29. Reginald T. Townsend, *Mother of Clubs: Being the History of the Union Club of the City of New York, 1839-1936* (New York: Union Club, 1936), 9.

30. Bellows, *Historical Sketch*, 38.

31. *The Century, 1847-1946* (New York: Century Association, 1947), 19.

32. Strong, *Diary of the Civil War*, 302.

33. Strong, *Diary of the Civil War*, 303.

34. Richard P. Phelan, "History Corner," Union League Club *Bulletin*, March 2004.

35. Strong, *Diary of the Civil War*, July 19, 1863.

36. David S. Reynolds, *Walt Whitman's America* (New York: Vintage, 1996), 424.

37. Lucy Gibbons Morse, "Personal Recollections of the Draft Riots of 1863," Peter Megagee Brown, *Riot of the Century* (New York: Trustees of the Riot Relief Fund, 1998), 41-49.

38. Iver Bernstein, *The New York Draft Riots: Their Significance for American Society and Politics in the Age of the Civil War* (New York: Oxford University Press, 1990), 55.

39. Herbert Asbury, *The Gangs of New York: An Informal History of the Underworld* (orig. publ. 1937). (New York: Random House Digital, 2008), 119.

40. *Report on the Committee on Volunteering* (New York: Union League Club, 1864), 4.

41. *Banquet Given by the Members of the Union League Club to Commemorate the Departure of the Seat of War of the Twentieth Regiment of United States Colored Troops Raised by the Club* (New York: 1886), 7.

42. George Washington Williams, *A History of the Negro Troops in the War of the Rebellion, 1861-1865* (New York: Harper & Brothers, 1887), 179.

43. John Rousmaniere, *Green Oasis in Brooklyn: The Evergreens Cemetery, 1849-2008* (Kittery, ME.: Seapoint Books, 2008), 120-22.

44. "Civil War Colored Troops Units with New York Soldiers of Officers," http://dmna.state.ny.us/historic/reghist/civil/other/coloredTroops/coloredTroopsMain.htm

45. Ernest Duvergier de Hauranne, "From *Eight Months in America*." *Writing New York: A Literary* Anthology, ed. Philip Lopate (New York: Literary Classics of America, 1998), 250-54.

46. Strong, *Diary of the Civil War*, 575.

47. Union Square Park. http://www.nycgovparks.org/parks/unionsquarepark/monuments/913

48. Strong, *Diary of the Civil War*, 600.

49. Strong, *Diary of the Civil War*, 584.

50. Strong, *Diary of the Civil War*, 581-2.

51. *New York Times*, May 23, 1867.

52. Bellows, *Historical Sketch*, 104.

53. John Jay, Introduction, Bayard Tuckerman, *William Jay and the Constitutional Movement for the Abolition of Slavery* (NY: Dodd, Mead, 1894), xvii-xviii.

54. Carrie Rebora Barratt, "*Washington Crossing the Delaware* and the Metropolitan Museum." *The Metropolitan Museum of Art Bulletin*, Fall 2012, 5-19.

55. H.T. Tuckerman, *Book of the Artists*, 1867, 11-12.

56. Winifred Eva Howe and Henry Watson Kent, *A History of the Metropolitan Museum of Art* (New York: Giliss Press, 1913), 101.

57. Will Irwin, Earl Chapman May, and Joseph Hotchkiss, *A History of the Union League Club of New York City* (New York: Dodd, Mead, 1952), 89.

58. Calvin Tompkins, *Merchants and Masterpieces: The Story of the Metropolitan Museum of Art* (New York: Holt, 1989).

59. *New York Times*, Jan. 14, 1899, Jan. 12, 1908.

60. Alexander B. Callow Jr., *The Tweed Ring* (New York: Oxford University Press, 1965), 266.

61. Callow, *Tweed Ring*, 83.

62. Kenneth D. Ackerman, *Boss Tweed: The Rise and Fall of the Corrupt Pol Who Conceived the Soul of Modern New York* (Berkeley: Carroll & Graf, 2006), 37.

63. Thomas Nast St. Hill, introduction, *Thomas Nast's Christmas Drawings* (New York: Dover, 1978), vi.

64. *Harper's Weekly*, August 26, 1871.

65. Albert Bigelow Paine, *Th. Nast: His Period and His Pictures* (New York: Macmillan, 1904), 134.

66. Edwin G. Burrows and Mike Wallace, *Gotham: A History of New York City to 1898* (New York: Oxford University Press, 1999), 1034.

67. Chauncey M. Depew, *Orations, Addresses, and Speeches of Chauncey M. Depew*, ed. John Denison Champlin (New York: 1910), 101.

68. Yasmin Sabin Kahn, Enlightening the World: The Creation of the Statue of Liberty (Ithaca: Cornell University Press, 2011), 135.

69. Esther Schor, *Emma Lazarus* (New York: Schocken, 2006), 191.

70. Richard P. Phelan, "History Corner," Union League Club *Bulletin*, April 2002.

71. Irwin, *History*, 279.

72. Bellows, *Historical Sketch*, 96.

73. Bellows, *Historical Sketch*, 96.

74. Irwin, *History*, 64. Strong, *Civil War Diary*, 416, 426.

75. *New York Times*, Feb. 18, 1879.

76. Francis Gerry Fairfield, *Clubs of New York, With an Account of the Origin, Progress, Present Condition, and Membership of the Leading Clubs; an Essay on New York Club-Life, and Photographs of Leading Club-Men* (New York: Hinton, 1873), 112.

77. Irwin, *History*, 258.

78. Strong, *Diary*, vol. 4, 203.

79. Bellows, *Historical Sketch*, 73.

80. Fairfield, *Clubs of New York*, 112. *New York Times*, Mar. 20, 1938.

81. Fairfield, *Clubs of New York*, 14, 117.

82. "New York as a Capital," *Scribner's*, Mar. 1890, 396.

83. *American Architect and Building News*, Apr. 26, 1879, 133-4.

84. Wheaton Arnold Holden, *Robert Swain Peabody of Peabody and Stearns in Boston, the Early Years (1870-1886).* Boston University, Ph.D. dissertation, 1969, 111.

85. "Some of the Union League's Decorations," *The Century*, vol. 23, no. 5 (Mar. 1882), 745 .Robert A.M. Stern, Thomas Mellins, and David Fishman, New York 1880: Architecture and Urbanism in the Gilded Age (New York: Monacelli, 1999), 188.

86. Stern, *New York 1880*, 188.

87. "Boston Architects," Great American Architects Series, no. 5, *Architectural Record*, July 1896, 72.

88. *New York Times*, Dec. 2, 1881.

89. Irvin, *History*, 219.

90. *New York Times*, Jan. 20, 1931.

91. Fairfield, *Clubs of New York*, 113.

92. *Time*, Oct. 6, 1941.

93. *New York Times*, June 18, 1994. *Autobiography of Mark Twain* (Berkeley: University of California Press, 2010), vol.1, 583. Information provided by Bonnyeclaire Smith-Stewart, Tucker, Ga., to Steele W. Hearne, April 27, 2012.

94. *New York Times*, Jul. 19, 1911.

95. *New York Times*, May 21, 1880.

96. Elizur Brace Hinsdale, *Autobiography with Reports and Documents* (New York: J.J. Little, 1901).

97. David C. Hammack, *Power and Society: Greater New York at the Turn of the Century* (New York: Columbia University Press, 1982), 313. Union League Club *Yearbook*, 1889, 55.

98. Irwin, *History*, 80.

99. Irwin, *History*, 82.

100. Irwin, *History*, 147.

101. Richard P. Phelan, "History Corner," Union League Club *Bulletin*, May 1998.

102. Theodore Roosevelt, *Theodore Roosevelt's Diaries of Boyhood and Youth* (New York: Scribner, 1928), 227.

103. Theodore Roosevelt, *Autobiography* (New York: Macmillan, 1913).

104. David McCullough, *Mornings on Horseback* (New York: Simon & Schuster, 1981), 138-39, 368, 370.

105. Theron George Strong, *Joseph H. Choate: New Englander, New Yorker, Lawyer, Ambassador* (New York: Dodd Mead, 1917), 66.

106. http://newyorkcitystatues.com/david-farragut/

107. Theodore Roosevelt, *The Letters of Theodore Roosevelt*, Ed. Elting E. Morison, et al. (Cambridge: Harvard University Press, 1951), vol. 1, 55.

108. Philip C. Jessup, *Elihu Root* (New York: Dodd, Mead, 1938), vol. 1, 70.

109. Irwin, *History*, 123.

110. Owen Wister, *Roosevelt: The Story of a Friendship, 1880-1919* (New York: Macmillan, 1930), 161-2.

111. McCullough, *Mornings on Horseback,* 314, 306.

112. Theodore Roosevelt, *New York* (London: Longmans Green, 1891), 211.

113. Jacob Riis, *The Making of an American* (New York: Macmillan, 1901), Chapter 13.

114. Richard Zachs, *Island of Vice: Theodore Roosevelt's Doomed Quest to Clean Up Sin-Loving New York* (New York: Doubleday, 2012), 204, 361.

115. *New York Times*, Feb. 7, 1938.

116. Edward Sandford Martin, *The Life of Joseph Hodges Choate as Gathered Chiefly from His Letters* (New York: Scribner, 1921), vol. 2, 72.

117. Joseph H. Choate, et al., *Speeches Delivered at the Banquet to Hon. Joseph H. Choate, Ambassador to England. Union League Club, Feb. 19, 1899.*

118. Jean Strouse, *Morgan: American Financier* (New York: Random House, 1999), 436.

119. Theodore Roosevelt, *Theodore Roosevelt's Letters to His Children* (New York: Scribner, 1919), Feb. 6, 1904.

120. *New York Times*, March 5, 1904.

121. Jessup, *Elihu Root*, vol. I , 416.

122. *New York Times*, Apr. 15, 1942. Another version of this story is in Irwin, *History*, 97-99.

123. Henry F. Pringle, *The Life and Times of William Howard Taft* (New York: Farnum and Rinehart, 1939), vol. 2, 898. Edmund Morris, *Colonel Roosevelt* (New York: Random House, 2010), 467.

124. Elihu Root, "Theodore Roosevelt," *North American Review*, December 1919, vol. 210, 754-5.

125. Union League Club *Yearbook*, 1917, 55.

126. Henry Pomeroy Davison, The American Red Cross in the Great War (New York: Macmillan, 1919), chapter 1. http://www.ourstory.info/library/2-ww1/Davison/rc1.html

127. Merlo J. Pusey, *Charles Evans Hughes* (New York: Macmillan, 1951), vol. 1, 368.

128. W.W. Brands, *T.R.: The Last Romantic* (New York: Basic Books, 1997), 779.

129. Irwin, *History*, 188.

130. Strong, *Joseph H. Choate*, 101-2.

131. Irwin, *History*, 189.

132. Jessup, *Elihu Root*, vol. 2, 327.

133. Union League Club *Yearbook*, 1919, 91.

134. Union League Club *Yearbook*, 1919, 61-2.

135. *New York Times*, Jul. 15, 2012.

136. Elihu Root, et al., *Elihu Root: Speeches Given at the Dinner Given at the Union League Club to Celebrate the Eightieth Anniversary of his Birth, Friday, February 13th, 1925* (Union League Club, 1925), 20.

137. Baltimore *Afro-American*, Feb. 7, 1931.

138. Arthur W. Little, *From Harlem to the Rhine: The Story of New York's Volunteers* (New York: Covici Friede, 1936), 115, 109, 110.

139. Little, *From Harlem to the Rhine*, 46-7.

140. *New York Age*, Sep. 10, 1938.

141. William Hayward, "A Tribute to My French General," *North American Review*, vol. 209, January-June 1919, 614.

142. John J. Pershing, *My Experiences in the World War* (New York: Stokes, 1931), vol. 2, 79.

143. Hayward, "A Tribute," 615.

144. Reid Badger, *Life in Ragtime: A Biography of James Reese Europe* (New York: Oxford University Press, 1995), 167.

145. Stephen L. Harris, *Harlem's Hell Fighters: The African-American 369th Infantry in World War I* (Washington: Brassey, 2003), 202, 225.

146. Little, *From Harlem to the Rhine*, 335.

147. Union League Club *Yearbook*, 1919, 54.

148. *New York Age*, Jul. 5, 1924.

149. Thomas W. Lamont, *Henry P. Davison: The Record of a Useful Life* (New York: Harper, 1933), 83.

150. Ron Chernow, *The House of Morgan* (New York: Atlantic Monthly, 1990), 144, 217.

151. Davison, *American Red Cross*, chapter 2.

152. Davison, *American Red Cross*, chapter 2.

153. *New York Times*, Dec. 1, 1918.

154. Jessup, *Elihu Root*, vol. 2, 477.

155. Union League Club *Yearbook*, 1921.

156. *Elihu Root: Speeches Given at the Dinner*, 17.

157. David E. Kyvig, *Repealing National Prohibition* (Chicago: University of Chicago Press, 1979), 17.

158. Union League Club *Yearbook*, 1931, 77-78.

159. *New York Times*, Feb. 25, 1931.

160. *New York Times*, Feb. 24, 1931.

161. *New York Herald-Tribune*, Feb. 15, 1931.

162. Jessup, *Elihu Root*, vol. 2, 477.

163. Irwin, *History*, 270-71.

164. Union League Club *Yearbook*, 1938, 66.

165. Irwin, *History*, 135. Charles H. Baker Jr., *The Gentleman's Companion, or Around the World with Jigger, Beaker, and Flask* (1939).

166. Minutes of Club meeting, Feb. 26, 1929. Union League Club archives.

167. Minutes, Feb. 26, 1929. Irwin, *History*, 213.

168. Robert A.M. Stern, Gregory Gilmartin, and Thomas Mellins, *New York 1930: Architecture and Urbanism between the Two World Wars* (New York: Rizzoli, 1987), 633, 624.

169. Matthew A. Postal, "Union League Club," Landmarks Preservation Commission report, Oct. 25, 2011, 6.http://www.nyc.gov/html/lpc/downloads/pdf/reports/2389.pdf

170. Rodger Friedman, "The Union League Club Clubhouse & Collection," 1995, 3. Union League Club archives.

171. Irwin, *History*, 173.

172. *New York Herald-Tribune*, Feb. 15, 1931.

173. Geoffrey T. Hellman and James Thurber, The Talk of the Town, "New House," *The New Yorker*, Feb. 7, 1931, p. 11.

174. Union League Club *Yearbook*, 1931, 56-57.

175. *New York Times*, Jan. 27, 1932 and Jan. 28, 1932.

176. *New York Times*, Jun. 5, 1930.

177. Irwin, *History*, 234.

178. Irwin, *History*, 227.

179. *New York Times*, Dec. 25, 1936.

180. Union League Club *Yearbook*, 1939, 65.

181. *New York Times*, May 2, 1937, Sep. 23, 1941. *Time*, Oct. 6, 1941.

182. *New York Age*, Sep. 10, 1938.

183. *New York Times*, May 2, 1937.

184. Richard P. Phelan, "History Corner," Union League Club *Bulletin*, June 2000.

185. Irwin, *History*, 219.

186. James M. Mayo, *The American Country Club: Its Origins and Development* (New Brunswick: Rutgers, 1998).

187. Irwin, *History*, 281-84.

188. Irwin, *History*, 260.

189. Irwin, *History*, 265.

190. Susan Hertog, *Dangerous Ambition: Dorothy Thompson and Rebecca West* (New York: Ballantine, 2011), 239.

191. *New York Times*, May 2, 1937.

192. *New York Times*, May 2, 1937.

193. Clarence Day, *Life with Father* (New York: Knopf, 1935), 207. See Katherine B. Day, "Living 'Life with Father': The Widow of Clarence Day Tells of the Creation of What Has Become an American Classic," *New York Times*, Nov. 5, 1939

194. Day, *Life with Father,* 11.

195. *New York Times*, Dec. 9, 1942.

196. "Talk of the Town," *New Yorker*, Apr. 1, 1944, 19.

197. Data in Union League Club *Yearbook*, 1945, 58-61, and 1947, 58.

198. Union League Club *Yearbook*, 1957, 60.

199. Union League Club *Yearbook*, 1960, 64.

200. John Willig, "Lament for the Male Sanctuary," *New York Times Magazine,* Mar. 10, 1957.

201. Union League Club *Yearbook*, 1957, 56-64.

202. *New York Times*, Mar. 30, 1952.

203. *New York Times*, Dec. 13, 1986.

204. Coates, Charles C. and Richard S. Stark. *Story of a Century*. Recording. New York: Union League Club /RCA-Victor, 1963.

205. Union League Club *Yearbook*, 1964, 60.

206. *Time*, Aug. 31, 1962.

207. *New York Times*, Dec. 23, 1983.

208. Jacquelin Carnegie, "Neighborhood," *Avenue*, December-January 1980, 54-55.

209. *New York Times*, Sep. 14, 1988.

210. *New York Times*, Mar. 26, 1983.

211. Union League Club *Yearbook*, 1987, 68, and 1988, 69-70.

212. Union League Club *Yearbook*, 1987, 76.

213. Albert T. Quantz Jr. to members, Jul. 26, 1988. Union League Club Archives.

214. *New York Times*, Feb. 24, 1891.

215. *New York Times*, Apr. 15, 1942.

216. Richard P. Phelan, "History Corner," Union League Club *Bulletin*, May 2003.

217. Andrea L. Chaffin, "John Sams in N.Y.C. Race." Clinton County News Journal, Jun. 28, 2012. http://wnewsj.com/main

Index

Union League Club President David Mathus and other members
celebrate the Club's 150th anniversary by closing the New York Stock Exchange on March 8, 2013.